"You're Joe's boy, ain't ya?"

"I was impressed with the eloquent simplicity of the lessons and the importance of their meaning."

Dave Draz, President
DiDit Enterprises

"I absolutely love the concept...you have a great ability to build suspense, tension and drive your lesson home."

Tom Belshe, Community Manager
Greater Arizona Development Authority

"After I read the first chapter, I put off something I needed to do so I could finish the rest. I think you have a winner."

David L. Bates, H.R. Manager
Avesta Sheffield

"I love the stories and images. There really is a life lesson in each chapter."

Lisa Ford, Owner
Ford Group, Inc.

"Heart warming stories we can all relate to. Made me smile and made me reflect back upon my own life and about what situations might have molded me into the person I am today and why."

Jodi Maynard, Customer Service Manager
SC Johnson Professional

You're Joe's boy, ain't ya?
Life's Lessons for Living, Loving & Leading

by Phillip Van Hooser, CSP

Phillip Van Hooser, CSP
Van Hooser Associates, Inc.
Post Office Box 643
Princeton, KY 42445
(270) 365-1536 • Fax (270) 365-6678
E-mail: phil@vanhooser.com
Web: www.vanhooser.com or www.joesboy.com

Editor: Al Borowski, MEd, CSP
Priority Communication Skills, Inc.
Pittsburgh, Pennsylvania

Cover Design: Karen Fulford
Beech Multimedia & Design, Inc.
Ocala, Florida

Library of Congress Catalog Card Number: 99-60245

ISBN 1-893322-43-2

Printed in the United States of America

ACKNOWLEDGEMENTS

If you believe an undertaking that requires a significant amount of time and effort, such as writing a book, can be accomplished by a single individual, you should go ahead and skip this section. However, you would be wrong to do so. Some may foolishly believe that because my name is the only one on the cover, I, therefore, deserve all the credit. The very thought is ridiculous. In the three years since I began this book, literally scores of people have contributed to its completion. I would like to take this opportunity to thank them.

To the hundreds of organizations and tens of thousands of individual audience members who have inspired me and confirmed the value of my message by hiring me and applauding my efforts since 1988, I sincerely thank you.

To individuals who went out of their way to provide an environment conducive to my writing. Folks like Rev. Phillip Hanes of First Baptist Church, Ocala, Florida, who provided a stash of soft drinks and Mr. Goodbars; Chief Rick Overman and Patty Taylor of the Delray Beach (FL) Police Department who secured a beachfront location for the writing to begin and finally, to Jeff Walker, Maile Deasy and the wonderful staff of Perry's Ocean-Edge Resort, Daytona Beach, Florida, for Room 519; to each of you, you have been wonderful.

To each of the individuals mentioned in the pages of this book, you are there because you have graced my life. For those written about who are no longer with us, their memory lives on in my mind and my heart.

To a number of special friends who took the time to read and offer feedback on the book while it was in process. Your insights, suggestions and words of encouragement were energizing. The list includes: Bob Ramey, Bob Mooneyham, Charles Dygert, Charles Petty, Dave Bates, Dave Draz, Dave Kratzer, Donald Dillon, Georgia Foley, Hugh Howton, Jay Akridge, Jerry Brenda, Jodi Maynard, Joe Calloway, Kent Foster, Linda Wheeler, Lisa Ford, Lou Heckler, Mal Lehman, Mansel Guerry, Martin Ramsay, Michael Philpot, Michael Smith, Nido Qubein, Patricia Fripp, Ray Pelletier, Rodger DeRose, Rosita Perez, Steve Garris, Tom Belshe, Tom Moser and Walter Bechtold.

To a wonderful friend and marvelous speaker who dedicated many hours to the process of editing the manuscript that became this book. Whatever this book is, it is better because of the involvement of Al Borowski, Priority Communication Skills, Inc., Pittsburgh, Pennsylvania.

To Jerry Hensley, my friend and former high school teacher, who challenged me to think beyond my horizons as a student more than twenty-five years ago. Thank you for your example, your faith in me and the wonderful foreword for this book.

To my brothers, Mark and Dan and my sister, Ellen, I am so proud of what you have become. I am even prouder to have witnessed you become it. Thank you for your patience, tolerance, forgiveness, love and support. You have helped me live longer, love better and laugh louder.

To Mom, whose love has always been unconditional. I have tried to remember who I am. Thanks for giving me a model to work toward.

To Kim Mercer, a trusted friend, who has offered coaching, counseling and cajoling throughout the past three years. Without her many efforts, the book may never have been completed.

To my kids, Joe, Sarah and Sophie who have tolerated absences related to my frequent writing retreats. You three have made my life richer than I could have ever dreamed. You are my joy.

To my wonderful wife, Susan, no one else could have done what you have done. Thank you for the love, support and unfailing commitment that have been with me every day through this project and through our time together. I love you and I'm thankful for you.

Finally, to Daddy. You are gone, but not forgotten.

FOREWORD

A common truism is that we never stop learning, but most of the important things that we learn come with the lessons of life. Although the facts and values that we learn as we are growing up help us develop and become the people we are, the truths learned in maturity hone us and take the rough edges off our being. Even though having a wonderful, loving family and a cadre of friends is beneficial in growing up, they are just as important in adulthood or maybe more so because usually we become less flexible as we grow older. A loving family living in a small town set into motion the learning process that stretches from childhood to adulthood for Phillip Van Hooser.

It has been my privilege to have known the entire Joe Van Hooser family for the past thirty years. During that time, I have also learned from this wonderful family. This is a family rooted in a strict agrarian society of western Kentucky. Hard work and strong family ties helped mold the Van Hooser children. The Van Hooser family was so accomplished, though, that it was hard to overlook a single one of them. They lived by example and others learned from the examples, especially Phillip.

Phillip's learning process as a youth and as an adolescent is reinforced by his mother's hard work, brother's and sister's support, small town relationships, and the deep-rooted values laid down by his father. During Phillip's childhood his father was constantly working Phillip and his brother, Mark, as if they were young mules that might amount to something one day, if he juggled firmness and fairness in training them. The boys were definitely bright, but also stubborn. Joe Van Hooser knew this and had to be firm with his boys. He also knew he was in charge of quality with Phillip and Mark and he wanted to train them just right. Phillip, especially, questioned his father's techniques, but never lost respect for him. Joe, though, appreciated his family and their desire for excellence, however, Joe was the father and there was no doubt about his place at the head of the family.

As Phillip reached adulthood he became more aware of his father's intentions—success. Phillip (not unlike most young adults) worried that perhaps his father had misunderstood his rebellion and he was not ready to stand alone as an independent adult. Knowledge acquired little by little led Phillip to know his father. Joe and Barbara had created an individual who would accomplish great things and bring honor to both of them. Phillip's lectures, writings and motivational workshops provide inspiration for both businesses and individuals. Everyday, some memory of his boyhood in Princeton, Kentucky, is used to emphasize the importance of finding strength inside oneself.

Father's and son's love, knowledge, hope and values transfer from one generation to the next. Joe imparted all these to his children and they in turn will give these gifts to their children. The first novel is indeed a tribute to Joe and his boy.

Jerry Hensley

DEDICATION

To my father,
Joseph Phillip Van Hooser.

His life: 1927-1987
His impact: Immense
His memory: Undying

INTRODUCTION

My most important lessons were learned outside a formal classroom. My most influential teachers were not formal educators at all. Though I have earned two formal educational degrees, my favorite classroom has been life itself. The best teachers? Just regular men and women I have encountered along my journey.

For years, I have shared my message of personal and professional commitment, courage and common sense with hundreds of thousands of individuals. Until now, my message has been communicated by way of the spoken word, through my role—my calling—as a professional speaker. More than eighteen hundred times I have stood before audiences to share valuable principles illustrated with lessons from life. Following programs, countless audience members have asked if my stories were available in written form. They haven't been, until now.

I began writing this book like I begin developing any speech or presentation. I began with the title: *"You're Joe's boy, ain't ya? Life's Lessons for Living, Loving and Leading."* Some readers may be curious about the title and what it represents.

Where I grew up in rural western Kentucky, like it or not, a person's identity was tied directly to who his or her parents were. If I introduced myself as Phillip Van Hooser, the common, even predictable response was, "Whose boy are ya?" or "You're Joe and Barbara's boy, ain't ya?"

Well, as it turns out, that's exactly who I am. Joe and Barbara's boy. I have come to realize that much of *what* I am is a direct result of *whose* I am. Much of what I know is a direct result of from whom I've learned it.

"You're Joe's boy, ain't ya?" consists of sixteen separate lessons or chapters, divided equally into four sections. *Growin' Up:* A collection of stories related to lessons learned as a child. *Learnin' How:* A collection of stories related to lessons learned as an adolescent. *Steppin' Out:* A collection of stories related to lessons learned as a young adult. *Movin' On:* A collection of stories related to lessons learned on my journey to manhood. Each chapter revolves around a single story. A story that ended up teaching me something I was able to use then *and*

later in life.

The stories are true, or at least as true as my memory of the last thirty-five years will allow them to be. The people are real. That's why I have written about them. I am impressed by honesty, integrity and unpretentiousness. Most importantly, the stories are written from my heart.

I hope they touch yours.

You're Joe's boy, ain't ya?

By Phillip Van Hooser

You're Joe's boy, ain't ya?

Life's Lessons for Living, Loving and Leading

Growin' Up

Learnin' How

Steppin' Out

Movin' On

Growin' Up

"Everywhere you trip is where your treasure lies."

NORMAN LEAR

- **Always Get Boot**

- **Watch Mammy**

- **I Gotta Go**

- **The Scarlet Letter**

1

Always Get Boot

"Boot." One of my father's favorite words. I have heard it used by him hundreds of times, but primarily in one specific context.

Over the years, I have found that when I have chosen to follow in my father's verbal footsteps and use his word in conversation, I am often met with that confused look that gives immediate indication that communication has been attempted, but understanding has not resulted.

My experience shows that most people define this simple word in one of the more traditional ways:

1) Boot: *Some sort of footwear, usually constructed of leather or rubber.*

   Example: As folks would say back in my part of Kentucky, "I've got a hole in my hip boots."

2) Boot: *To kick with the foot.*

   Example: "Things were going pretty good for the Braves until the shortstop booted the ground ball in the eighth inning."

3) Boot: *To be dismissed without much afterthought.*

   Example: "The smartest thing she ever did was to give that old boy the boot."

All of these definitions are perfectly acceptable and probably somewhat familiar. But, they were not the way Joe Van Hooser chose to use the word. For him, the word was much more important. The simple word "boot" rang with opportunistic clarity.

You see, if nothing else, my father was a trader. He had

been from his childhood. He simply loved the process of bargaining with and for things. Over the years, I learned that material goods held little sentimental value for him. From his vantage point, virtually everything was open to and available for a trade. So the word "boot," especially the way Mr. Webster chose to define it, fit my father's purposes nicely.

Boot: *Something to equalize a trade.*

If it had to do with a trade, Daddy knew about it. He was constantly in search of that great equalizer—boot.

In the formative years of my youth, I spent a lot of time with my father. From age five or so, when Daddy was not working, my younger brother and I would accompany him almost everywhere. This constant companionship was both by choice and necessity. On occasion, it proved to be both monotonous and educational.

During the long winter months, Daddy often found himself laid off from his construction painting jobs. My mother worked outside the home. Therefore, by necessity, my brother, Mark, and I got to tag along with Daddy.

One of our almost daily stops was the local courthouse. My hometown, Princeton, Kentucky, is the seat of government for rural Caldwell County. Like many small towns throughout the United States, and especially the South, our courthouse served as the geographic center of the business community.

Daddy loved the courthouse. He seemed irresistibly drawn to it. Not because of its geographic location or unique architectural design. No, my father loved the courthouse and its basement. Or more specifically, the activities that originated there.

In the massive two-story concrete structure that rose above the courthouse basement, the continuing business of local government and politics was carried out. These on-going activities were always popular topics of discussion with the patrons of the courthouse basement. Criticism and second-guessing of local politicians, regardless the significance of their decisions, were always popular activities. No matter the issue, in the end, everyone would agree that the decision could, as it was frequently stated, "hurt 'em (the politicians) at election time."

However, well beyond the trivial matters of politics and their impact, the basement dwellers had a life, a culture, a purpose all their own.

On any given day, Monday through Saturday, at any given time, between the hours of 8:00 a.m. and 4:30 p.m., middle aged and older men, numbering on average from three to twenty, gathered for two common purposes. Socialization and trading. Not necessarily in that order.

For these individuals, with time on their hands, the socialization process took one or more of the following forms. Some came prepared to whittle. Some came prepared to play checkers. Some came prepared to swap exaggerated hunting stories. But, almost all came prepared to trade. Smoking, chewing, napping and cussing were optional activities.

Daddy showed no interest at all in whittling or playing checkers and little interest in talking hunting. No, he was much more focused. The almost daily excursions to the courthouse basement served the sole purpose of allowing Daddy to see who was there and what they had to trade. For Joe Van Hooser, the next trade was the continuing allure.

Each day was a new adventure. What will be available today? A chain saw? A lemon colored, pointer birddog? Cedar corner posts? Concrete blocks from some long overdue demolition project? Or maybe a pocketknife.

My dad was open to trading for anything, as long as he got his "boot." However, by far, his favorite trading items were pocketknives. He, and most every other male of that generation, rarely were without a pocketknife. Therefore, when coming into contact with any other male, no matter where or why, a trade could be struck.

For us, these almost daily encounters always began the same. As we would arrive at the courthouse and start down the stairs leading to the basement, Daddy would stop and focus his full attention on my brother and me. His instructions were always the same. Instructions that had been offered dozens of times before. "Boys, listen here. No matter what happens or what's said down here, I don't want y'all to say a word. Just sit still and be quiet. We won't be here long."

The routine was always the same. After receiving our daily marching, or rather sitting orders, we would amble into the basement and begin the search for empty seats. On frosty winter mornings, the choices were severely limited. The county had seen fit to provide just two old wooden benches as the only permanent pieces of furniture. They sat on either side of the basement aisle, directly facing each other. One was strategically located next to the Coca-Cola and Tom's Peanuts vending machines. The other sat under the hand-lettered sign on the wall that sarcastically read:

"If you spit on the floor at home,
spit on the floor here.
We want you to feel at home."

If these "premium" seats were occupied, a curious variety of less desirable options were available. The options included an ever-changing combination of broken cane bottom chairs, empty five-gallon paint buckets, or old wooden Coke bottle crates. The crates were especially challenging in that they required highly advanced skills of balance and equilibrium to successfully operate. When worse came to worst, common on busy mornings, seatless basement dwellers were forced to lean or squat against cold, gray, marble basement walls until seats became available. Perpetual shifting was required to keep the blood from pooling in one foot or the other. Mark and I, by virtue of our tender ages and the supposed resilience that accompanies youth, were frequently volunteered as leaners and squatters.

I remember one particularly cold winter morning. The morning began like so many others. When we had arrived at the courthouse, received our instructions, greeted those assembled there and settled into the process of observing the panorama of activities surrounding us, Daddy began a series of trades that I will never forget.

While earnestly engaged in the business of cleaning his fingernails with his own pocketknife, Daddy directed a question to an aging gentleman seated next to him.

"Hoyt, what kinda knife ya got on ya?" my father casually asked.

"Oh, I've gotta pretty good 'un, Joe. A three bladed Old Timer. Why, what are you carryin'?"

"I've gotta a three blade, Case Double X with a bone handle. Not too heavy, but it'll still hold a good, sharp edge."

"Well, lemme have a look," Hoyt said, as he and my father exchanged knives.

For the next three minutes or so, the two veteran traders sat in silence as they examined each other's knives. For all practical purposes, the knives were identical. Not that they looked the same or were created by the same manufacturer. But, from an application standpoint, both knives had been designed to accomplish the same basic tasks. Additionally, the quality of materials and craftsmanship used to create both were basically the same—and both men knew it. As instructed, I watched silently, but with keen interest.

For some time, the silence raged uninterrupted. Both men intent in their evaluations. Both men plotting their strategies. Finally, the time came to begin trading in earnest. As always, the first step was to establish the perceived value of both knives by their respective owners.

"Whatta ya want for it?" Hoyt asked my father, without looking up.

"Oh, I don't wanna sell it," was Daddy's predictable reply.

It wasn't a lie. He didn't want to *sell* it. He wanted to trade. That's what drew us here on this frosty morning in the first place.

"If I sold it," Daddy went on, "I'd be without a knife." As he spoke, my father casually returned Hoyt's Old Timer to its rightful owner. Hoyt now sat, holding both knives. He paused briefly before speaking.

"Well then, Joe, how would ya trade?"

There it was!! The trade had officially begun. This was the part I enjoyed most. Even as a young boy, I could appreciate the give and take from these two cagey traders that was sure to follow.

"Positioning" is how professional sales and negotiation skills trainers might describe the process. This positioning activity could be completed quickly, or could conceivably continue for an indefinite period. Each trading participant seeking to wear down the other. The length of the positioning stage was dependent on variable factors such as the time available for the trade to be completed, the value of the trading item in question and simply put, the resolve of each trader. I have witnessed my father sit ten, twenty, even thirty minutes at a time, in total silence, facing his fellow trader, waiting for some indication, some opening from which to work his next negotiation point.

On this particular day, since the trade items in question were relatively insignificant, and since both traders knew that many other trade opportunities lay ahead before those basement doors would be locked later that afternoon, the positioning was brief and to the point.

"I'd hafta have your knife and seven dollars boot," Daddy calmly replied.

"Seven dollars! Why, your knife by itself ain't worth seven dollars!" Hoyt shot back quickly, knowing that his words were not true, but seeking to evoke an emotional response from his opponent.

Without offering a single word of defense on behalf of the old Case Double X, Daddy simply reached to retrieve the knife from Hoyt's grasp. Hoyt, however, was not quite ready to relinquish it.

"Joe Van Hooser, what makes ya think your knife is seven dollars better'n my Old Timer?" Hoyt asked directly, still clutching both knives.

"The main thing is that the spring in the big blade of your

old knife is loose. It's even loose to the touch." While Hoyt examined the blade, Daddy continued with his analysis. "The first time ya put the least little bit of pressure on that blade, it's apt to break. Then what'd it be worth? Anyway, I'm happy with my knife." He reached for the Case Double X again. Hoyt held on tightly.

After a few more questions and rebuttals, a deal was predictably struck. The knives were exchanged and pocketed by their new owners. In addition, my father pocketed his boot— the handsome, skillfully negotiated, sum of five dollars and change for his efforts. The entire episode had lasted no more than ten minutes. Both men parted friends, confident they had gotten the better end of the trade.

During the course of that same day, in that same courthouse basement, Daddy traded knives a total of ten more times. The participants changed, of course, with both Hoyt and my father having gone their separate ways in search of new opportunities. However, the trades themselves continued throughout the day, remaining remarkably similar, in process at least, to the earlier ones. With each trade, I saw my father pocket a new knife and his negotiated boot.

Finally, the time came to leave the courthouse and head for home. It had been a good day for me, watching Daddy at work. As we exited the dark, dank basement and stepped onto the sidewalk outside, safely out of earshot of the other basement patrons, Daddy stopped and turned his full attention to his boys.

"Boys, y'all were good in there today," he noted. "Before we leave, I wanna show ya somethin'."

He reached into his pocket and pulled out a fistful of bills and some change. Slowly, he counted it out in front of us. The total came to fifty-one dollars even. The impact was immediate. I was *very* impressed. Seldom had I seen that much money at one time. From my vantage point, it might as well have been fifty-one *hundred* dollars. He let the impact of the sight of the cash sink in. Finally, he spoke again.

"Lemme show y'all somethin' else."

With those words, he reached deeper into his pocket and retrieved the knife he had gotten during his last trade of the day. Both Mark and I recognized it immediately. It was his original Case Double X!! The very one with which he had started the day's trading activity. The very one that he had traded to Hoyt. Obviously, Hoyt had continued his trading activity on this day as well.

When he was sure we recognized the knife, he said, "Boys, always remember that when ya trade, whatever you're tradin' for, always trade up! Things are always more valuable to folks when they don't own 'em yet. It's your job to show 'em why they need 'em. But, once push comes to shove, don't waste your time tradin' even. Always get boot!"

As I think back on it now, that proved to be a pretty good day for me. The memory of which has stayed with me all these years. Quality time spent with my father and brother and a timeless lesson on trading—to boot!

"The cynic is the one who knows the price of everything and the value of nothing."

OSCAR WILDE

2

Watch Mammy

The weather was miserable. The sky was depressingly gray. A bone chilling mist hung endlessly in the air. Maple, oak, elm and hickory trees stood barren along the roadside, their leaves having departed weeks before.

As unpleasant as it was outside, it would have been the perfect Saturday morning for this eight-year old to sit inside, wrapped in a worn quilt, watching Mighty Mouse cartoons and the adventures of my entire generation's Saturday morning friend, Flicka. But, not this Saturday morning. No, this Saturday morning found me and my brother, Mark, huddled against the cold in the cab of my dad's old green and white pickup truck. Daddy was at the wheel.

We were traveling through familiar territory. The eight mile drive from Princeton brought us eventually to the sign announcing entry into Farmersville, Kentucky. Instinctively, Daddy tapped the brakes lightly. A couple of hundred yards further, the only commercial structure in Farmersville came into sight—the Farmersville store.

As we slowed in front of this local center of commerce (assuming of course, that you were in the market for items such as milk, bread, fifty pounds of dog feed, fresh sliced bologna or a gallon of the twentieth century's miracle drug—turpentine), Daddy, while skillfully applying both clutch and brake, down shifting and executing a thirty degree left turn onto the adjoining gravel side road, quickly tooted the truck horn.

I instinctively looked for the intended recipient of this greeting. I noticed two aging gas pumps and the wooden bench on "the store's" front porch. But, no person in sight. His actions were just habit, I guessed.

"Daddy, where we going?" I heard Mark ask.

"To Ted McNeely's house," Daddy replied.

"Why?"

"He's got some calves I wanna take a look at."

Ted McNeely, "Teddy Bear" to his friends, lived off the gravel road that ran directly past the Donaldson Baptist Church, about two miles from the Farmersville store. A life long farmer, Ted raised cattle, hay and tobacco on a secluded piece of ground nestled between the tiny farming communities of Farmersville and Flat Rock.

Ted was ten to fifteen years older than my dad. They had known each other for years. From memory, I could recall Ted stopping by our house on various occasions. However, this would be the first time that I had been in his home.

I began to perk up at the thought of the visit. This early in the morning, Ted's wife, Almerine was sure to be preparing breakfast. Probably eggs, homemade country sausage and biscuits. She would insist that we eat.

After breakfast, I easily imagined Mark and I emerging from the house and traipsing around the muddy barnyard while Daddy and Ted talked trade. I began to realize that this might prove to be an enjoyable morning after all.

"Boys," Daddy's words interrupted my plans. "I want y'all to behave once we get to the house. Before ya go in, make sure that ya wipe your feet off good so that ya don't track mud into Almerine's kitchen."

These pre-arrival instructions were concise, to the point and totally predictable. We had heard them so often before that both Mark and I could have recited them by heart. We were also well aware that he meant every word.

"Oh, yeah, before I forget. I understand that Ted's momma ain't doin' real good."

His words sounded strange. Unusual. They caught both of us by surprise. One of us, I think Mark, spoke next.

"Ted's momma is still alive?" he asked curiously.

Since neither Mark nor I had ever seen her, I suppose we

both assumed that she was no longer living. After all, Ted and Almerine seemed ancient to us. (Probably in their 50's at the time.)

"Yep, she's still livin'," my dad replied.

"How old is she?" we both asked.

"Oh, I don't know for sure. Older than your granddaddy. I'd guess she's in her late 80's, maybe even 90," Daddy responded casually. Then he added, "But, from what I understand she ain't doin' good at all."

There, he said it again. It must be serious. She must be really sick. Curiosity quickly overcame us.

"Daddy, what's wrong with her?"

That's when he dropped the bombshell. Neither of us saw it coming.

"Miss Etney's losin' her mind," was my dad's straightforward reply.

We both froze. She what?! Immediately, Mark and I looked at each other, but did not speak. I didn't know what to think and certainly didn't know what to say. We were left to sit in silence and ponder his words and our thoughts.

Losing her mind? That means she's going crazy. Or, maybe she's already crazy! A gnawing fear began to creep into the pit of my stomach.

Lest you think that our father was being terribly insensitive to a very real human condition, let me remind you that thirty years ago, much less was known about the specific ravages of the aging process. Now, more than three decades later, even young children recognize and understand Alzheimer's for what it is—a disease. An apparently, incurable, irreversible and devastating mental condition. But, on that day, in the cab of that pickup truck, it was still an unknown and therefore, terribly frightening, concept.

As the fear and uncertainty began to grow perceptibly within us, I felt the truck slow and the tires bite into the loose gravel. As we made that final gradual right turn onto the long mud and limestone rock driveway, the McNeely house came into sight.

The house itself was like many others of that era in our part of the country. A fairly large, wooden frame structure, several years past needing a new coat of paint. The roof was tin with a number of chimneys protruding from it. The chimneys were necessary to accommodate the fireplaces or "grates" located throughout the house. These coal-burning grates heated most of the houses of that period.

As we rolled to a stop in front of the house, I hesitated before climbing down from the truck. I was not at all anxious to face my fears and the "crazy" woman who lived inside. Nevertheless, at Daddy's insistence, Mark and I slowly exited the truck and joined him on the steps leading up to the back porch. Suddenly, the screen door to the kitchen swung open and Ted emerged. Standing in faded overalls and sock feet, with his ever-present roll-your-own, Prince Albert tobacco cigarette dangling from his lips, he beckoned us in. As we entered the warm kitchen, as expected, Almerine was busy preparing the first meal of the day. Three additional place settings had already been arranged. Everything was exactly as I had imagined, except there was no sign of Miss Etney.

At Almerine's urging, Daddy conceded and the three of us joined Ted and Almerine for a country breakfast of eggs, sausage, biscuits and homemade sorghum molasses. The food was wonderful, but I couldn't enjoy a bite of it. I was too busy wondering where "she" was and what "she" was doing.

After several agonizing minutes of coffee and small talk, Ted rose from the table and announced that it was time to go have a look at those calves.

A feeling of immediate relief swept over me. Mark and I sprang to our feet and reached for our jackets. We were thrilled at the prospect of leaving this house. However, our ecstasy was short lived.

"Boys," Ted began. "I need y'all to stay in the house while me and Joe go look at 'em calves. Almerine needs to step out back and feed the chickens. (I now suspect these words to be Ted's code phrase for Almerine's morning trip to the outhouse.)

So, I need you boys to watch Mammy."

Watch Mammy?!

My heart stopped. I couldn't move. I could barely breathe. Desperately, I looked first to Mark who appeared to be in the same shape I was. I then looked helplessly to Daddy who seemed totally oblivious to our immediate plight.

All the while, Ted began herding us toward the big, closed door at the far end of the kitchen. As he walked, he continued to talk.

"Somebody's gotta stay in the house with Mammy all the time. If we don't, she tries to run off. We gotta watch her like a hawk. Just the other day, she got away from us and run off down through the field toward the creek. We liked to have never caught her. It's a wonder she didn't hurt herself. Don't worry though, she'll be glad to see y'all. She ain't around kids much."

Was that supposed to make us feel better?

To this day, I cannot remember a time during which I was more frightened. My imagination raced as Ted reached for the door handle that would provide entry into Miss Etney's room. It was here and now that my imagination would come face to face with reality.

As the heavy oak door swung open, a huge, imposing room immediately appeared. Ten-foot ceilings, with sparse furnishings and decorations made the room appear larger still. The window in the wall to the left served as the room's only source of natural light. In the adjoining wall was located the room's grate. A half-full coal bucket nearby, ready when necessary, to refuel the fire that crackled softly.

The room's furnishings were basic. A rocking chair sat between the grate and the window. Perfectly positioned to take full advantage of both warmth and light. On the opposite side of the grate sat a handmade chest of drawers. Mismatched pictures from a bygone era hung on the wall above it. On the floor were several "throw rugs" offering limited relief for bare feet from the cold linoleum they covered.

The primary piece of furniture, an oversized, four poster feather bed, sat against the wall facing the grate. On the bed was an assortment of faded quilts covering a bulging mattress. In the middle of the mattress perched Miss Etney.

I say perched, because my first recollection of her is that of some sort of strange bird. A slightly built woman, weighing one hundred pounds or less, she had big eyes and a long neck that she craned to enable her to see what was beneath and around her.

She sat statue still—except for occasional movements of her neck, head and eyes. Her arms were wrapped around her knees that she had drawn tightly to her breasts. She was dressed in a well-worn, full length, long sleeved, cotton gown. Her silky white hair was wild and retreating from her head in every direction.

She watched us closely.

And we watched her.

Ted began his instructions to us.

"Boy," he said, first taking, then leading Mark by the shoulder. "You stand over here in front of the winder." The window was big and looked out over the side yard and beyond to the pasture.

"Don't worry, Mammy won't try to get past ya."

Miss Etney sat, watching and listening.

Then turning his attention to me he said, "Son, you just stand here in front of this door after I close it. Boys, y'all just talk to Mammy and she'll be awright."

With those simple instructions, Ted and Daddy were gone, leaving the two of us to "watch Mammy."

We never got the chance to talk to her as instructed. As soon as the door had closed, Miss Etney started talking to us.

"Boys, they hate me," she began, as she looked quickly and wildly at first one and then the other of us. "They hate me. They won't let me go outside to see my friends. I miss my friends," she said, apparently referring to friends long since gone.

Her words were unsettling. But, even more so, her actions as she spoke them. With every word she became more and more energized and animated. In a matter of seconds she had repositioned herself and was now on her hands and knees in the middle of the bed. She faced us and continued to talk.

"You boys can help me see my friends. Won't ya please help me see my friends?"

Suddenly, she was out of the bed.

It was obvious she had few, if any, physical restrictions. As she quickly climbed down from the bed and stood on the cold floor beside it, she was noticeably small, but certainly not frail. Quick, but not aggressive.

Nevertheless, both Mark and I stood frozen in place. We simply didn't know what to do. As she rambled on, not waiting for or wanting any response from us, she began to move, even drift, toward the other side of the bed. In a matter of seconds, she stood facing the chest of drawers, directly between Mark and me.

As she reached the chest, with the two of us dutifully manning our sentry positions, she began to tug at the handles of the top drawer. When sufficiently open, she reached inside and to our horror, produced a claw hammer. Our previous fear and uncertainty gave way to unequaled terror. Would she attack?

Before we could make any physical attempt to either retreat or defend ourselves, Miss Etney lowered herself to her knees and began tugging at yet another drawer. The bottom one. I wondered "What tool of mutilation would it contain?"

After considerable effort, the drawer relented and slid open. To my surprise, I realized that it was stocked with a generous supply of hickory nuts. These "hicker nuts" were a regional delicacy, equal in local popularity to the more familiar pecans or walnuts.

With hammer in one hand and a generous supply of nuts now gathered in the lap of her gown, Miss Etney, calmly lowered herself to the floor, directly facing the crackling fire. Methodically, one after another of the nuts was strategically placed on the rock hearth before her. With a precision that comes only with practice, she carefully struck each nut with the hammer. Once the outer shells had been cracked, she would meticulously pick out the "hicker nut goodies" (the meat portion of the nut) and eat them, while continuing to ramble aimlessly about her imagined enemies, her forced incarceration and the need to see her friends.

Soon, it became clear that Miss Etney was no danger to us. She was simply an old lady whose mind was forsaking her. The final few minutes with Miss Etney, before Daddy and Ted returned, have proven to be one of my more lasting memories.

I have found that ignorance of the unknown too often serves as a fertile breeding ground for unfounded fears. If allowed to take root, such fears can grow to such a degree, that they eventually take full control of our thoughts and actions. To avoid such a dire outcome, I have come to realize fears must be confronted directly. In doing so, those fears are often exposed for what they truly are, gross exaggerations, created and fueled by overactive imaginations. Two young boys could attest to that.

———

"When the day is over and you've done your best, wait the results in peace."
JUDY MARSTON

3

I Gotta Go

Life in the Van Hooser household was fairly predictable, even routine. Some would say boring. I say foundation building. A lot of work, occasional play and always time for church. Usually, three times a week. Sunday morning, Sunday School and worship service. Sunday evening, Training Union and worship service. Wednesday evening, Prayer Meeting. In our spare time, we engaged in other church related activities including revival meetings, summer Bible Schools, graveyard cleanings and my personal favorite, the annual church wide "varmint supper." (That's another story for another day.)

I realize that some of these terms may be unfamiliar, or possibly totally foreign, to those readers not well versed in ways of Baptists. Every religious denomination creates its own accepted method of worship and the terminology to describe it. We Baptists have always seemed more comfortable with the frequency and variety of worship and fellowship activities than do many other denominations.

I fully accept that our ways are not for everybody. To be honest, sometimes even Baptists themselves have trouble with them. I once heard a Baptist preacher say that a former member of his congregation had explained her personal exodus from the local Baptist church to its Methodist counterpart across the street by saying, "I just didn't have the energy to be a Baptist anymore." Frankly, I can understand that. As a child, I grew up napping on church pews. I have feasted on the potluck offerings of innumerable "dinners on the grounds." While secular neighbors reveled and rang in each new year with rousing renditions of Auld Lang Syne, I joined my family and other church members in eating stale doughnuts and listening to southern gospel quartets perform at local "watch night" services.

Please don't misunderstand. I have very few unpleasant memories of my more than four decades of regular church attendance and involvement. My affiliation with the Baptist church and it's various activities has been instrumental in laying the Biblical foundation on which the structure of my faith is built. For my parent's unwavering commitment to exposing me to the spiritual side of existence, I will always be grateful.

As certain as I am that specific "Baptist terminology" may be unfamiliar, I am equally certain that the methodology of our worship experiences might be misunderstood as well.

Many people believe that all church worship experiences are like those frequently depicted on television. The visual images are clearly ingrained in most of us. Huge ornate temples, cathedrals, sanctuaries or auditoriums teeming with hundreds even thousands of devoted followers. Music runs the gamut from soft and sober, to loud and vibrant. Pastors, priests, rabbis and evangelists dressed in flowing robes or designer suits address spellbound congregation members. Some services are noteworthy for their structured solemnity, others by their spontaneous exuberance. I have seen many examples of all these. But, none of these accurately depict my early church experiences.

My formative years were spent worshiping in a little country church in Farmersville, Kentucky. Worship services at Donaldson Baptist Church were nothing like the flickering images depicted on television. There was no huge auditorium. The maximum capacity of our church building was probably no more than one hundred seventy-five. Not that it mattered. Capacity seating was seldom a concern. On special occasions, such as Christmas, Easter Sunday and during the occasional community wide revival service, overcrowding was only a remote possibility. Otherwise, one hundred or so of the faithful would be considered a "good turnout" on any typical Sunday morning. Significantly less for all evening and mid-week services.

The pastors who occupied the pulpit over the years at Donaldson Baptist Church were also very different from their televised counterparts. I never remember names like Dr. Thurston V. Soandso, III. Instead, we were spiritually led and fed by solid men with solid names like Brother Emerson, Brother Wyatt and Brother Riley. These shepherds did not address their flocks wearing elaborate outfits or shellacked hairdos. Their wives were so unassuming and nondescript that they could seldom be singled out from other parishioners.

For the most part, these were simple men and women who loved God and who had dedicated their lives to serving and sharing the Good News of Jesus Christ with their flocks. Because of their selfless, committed service, many people made life-changing decisions, in preparation for their eternal rewards. I know, because I was one. However, as a child I didn't always appreciate these servants and their work as I should have. Few of us did.

Even from a very early age, I can remember the order of a typical worship service. It varied little from Sunday to Sunday. The first hour of the morning was the Sunday School hour. This period focused on Bible study classes led by volunteer teachers from within the membership.

Sunday School was a joy for me. We always seemed to be learning about some wonderful, far away adventure. Giants— David and Goliath. Wild animals—Daniel in the lion's den. Adventures at sea—Jonah and the whale and Noah's Ark. Remarkable miracles—Jesus feeding the five thousand with five loaves and two fishes. Each story would end with a time of discussion and sharing, washed down with grape Kool-Aid and chocolate cookies. Besides being spiritually enlightening, it was great fun.

Immediately following Sunday School, folks would be encouraged to move toward the sanctuary for the mid-morning "preaching" service. With the piano playing softly in the background and the melody drifting through the open windows of the auditorium to the church grounds and fields beyond, people would begin making their way in.

First, the older members of the congregation would shuffle to the seats that some of them had religiously occupied for decades. This gray brigade would be followed closely by young families arriving early to stake out seats for extended family and friends. As they positioned themselves on their chosen pews, babies in tow would cry loudly and often, in the absence of a church nursery. Giggling adolescents would group awkwardly together on the back few pews of the church, hopefully, well out of the line of sight of their peering parents. Gradually, the empty pews would begin to fill with mothers, grandmothers, teenagers and squirming children.

The last to arrive were the men, both young and old. Hard working, God fearing, salt of the earth type men. Men who made their living with their hands and their backs, but, who prayed with their hearts and souls. Painters, carpenters, laborers and farmers. Some fresh from their last cigarette or their last chaw of tobacco. As these men ambled toward their waiting families, many would retrieve handkerchiefs from their hip pockets and work to wipe away the tobacco spittle, known as ambeer, still glistening in the wrinkles of the corner of their mouths.

Our church was the oldest established Baptist church in Caldwell County. Built long before the luxuries of air conditioning and indoor plumbing were available to common folks, large windows often stood open wide, hoping to attract some cool breeze, which in turn might offer some respite from the stifling mid-summer humidity. In the absence of such a breeze, congregation members would search the hymnal racks looking for one of the complimentary Morgan's Funeral Home hand fans strategically positioned there. Soon, fans would flutter crisply back and forth throughout the auditorium. The rapid movement of the fans served to create an artificial breeze and to shoo away the flies the open windows had attracted. In such an environment, one could literally see, hear, smell and feel the realities of a rural worship experience.

Because our congregation was so small, we had no established choir and no formal choir robes. Each service began with the pianist (no organ, orchestra or soundtrack) playing softly some prelude to worship chosen from the Broadman Hymnal. There were no paid staff members assigned the formal titles of "choir director," "music minister," or "worship leader." The closest thing we had was a dedicated middle aged farmer named Otis. Otis served the dual capacity as both "song leader" and janitor—not necessarily in that order of importance. Both positions were voluntary and therefore, unpaid ones. Otis' formal musical training was non-existent and his performing talent similar. However, what he lacked in musical skills, he more than made up for in faith, commitment and volume. Regardless of weather conditions, conflicting priorities or personal inconvenience, Otis was not just there "whenever the doors were open," Otis was responsible for opening those doors!

With the piano continuing to play, Otis would eventually leave his seat on the front pew and amble slowly and deliberately forward. Climbing the three steps up to the platform, Otis would methodically station himself behind the solid oak pulpit. Once in this position, Otis would begin to beckon, encourage and even beg members to leave the comfort and relative anonymity of their pews and join him in the "choir." The "choir loft" consisted of two rows of folding chairs positioned on the raised platform facing both the congregation and Otis' rear end. Those responding to the call would serve as that service's ad hoc choir.

As the begging began to wear on the consciences of various individuals, slowly one by one, men and women would rise from their seats and move forward, allowing that morning's choir to take shape. With all assembled, the number seldom exceeded twelve. The group was made up of all shapes and sizes with little formal order to their arrangement. No alto or tenor sections. Simply men in the back and women up front. Once the hymn selection was announced, members of the congregation and choir alike were encouraged to "jump in and sing out." More often than not, we did.

The choir would lead the congregation in three or four songs with brief interludes for prayer, announcements, the welcome of any visitors and the "passing of the plate" for the collection of that week's "tithes and offerings." With their service complete, the choir members were excused and encouraged to return to their original seats to rejoin their friends and families. Soon after, the preaching service would begin.

Sunday after Sunday this scene played itself out. Certainly there were variations. On occasion, the pulpit would be surrendered to a guest temperance speaker or some missionary doing God's work in some mysterious, far-flung location like Africa, China or Utah. But, the variations were few. And I loved it.

As a young boy, I made a game of guessing who would be cajoled into singing in the choir on any given Sunday. I loved singing along, loudly and over time could do so by heart. I loved the physical activity of sitting, standing and then sitting again at various points in the service. I especially enjoyed shaking hands and getting hugs from family, friends and visitors alike during the visitor welcoming period.

However, I must admit, once the preaching service got under way, my attention span grew short. The auditorium would become noticeably quieter. Where only moments before we had been encouraged to make a "joyful noise," I was now expected to sit quietly for the next thirty to forty-five minutes. As the preacher began to explore the intricacies of the scriptures, I would begin to drift mentally away.

My dad didn't have a great number of church rules that required regular review. We all were imminently aware of those few things that he simply would not tolerate. Mom had rules, too. But, her rules were applied with a compassionate mother's heart. Under certain circumstances, she would practice leniency. Daddy, however, was different. When Daddy's rules were broken (or even bent a little bit) Joe Van Hooser showed no leniency and often, no heart.

What wouldn't he tolerate in church? Misbehaving! A somewhat vague term that he alone would define. For him, it was simple. A church service was to be approached with a solemn, respectful attitude. Disruptions and distractions of any type, by his children, would not be tolerated. Never mind that there almost always seemed to be some sort of disruptive commotion under way around us. Babies crying, songbooks falling and even an occasional snort from some dozing member of the congregation. If one of us kids so much as sneezed too aggressively, Daddy would respond with a snap of the fingers, a sharp thump on the head, or "the look." You know what I'm talking about. Every parent has their own version of "the look." I'm convinced that children around the world can recognize it instantly.

Though the rules were well understood, occasionally even the most obedient child would choose to test the boundaries. After all, how can one be certain of exactly where the boundaries are if they are not stepped over occasionally? Since I was far from being the most obedient child, I was always on the lookout for loopholes—a foolproof way of skirting the established order of things. On one occasion, I thought I had found one.

The only barely acceptable reason for getting up and leaving a church service in progress was unexpected illness. Though an occasional reality, even responding to nature's call was not an acceptable excuse. We all knew it. Constantly, we kids were reminded to "go" before every service.

Quite by accident, one Sunday morning, just as the choir was released from their voluntary service, I felt nature's urge. Fearing some unspeakable accident during the preaching service, Mom quickly took me by the hand and led me out. All eyes were fixed on us. Self-righteous mothers silently wondering why Barbara Van Hooser didn't have better control of her children. Envious children silently wishing they had less control of their bladders and the temporary reprieve a bathroom break would provide.

Once out the back door of the auditorium and out from under the unrelenting gaze of other members, Mom herded me quickly toward the back door of the church building and down the winding, overgrown path to the nondescript outhouse that serviced such emergencies.

The outhouse itself was an adventure. Not that I was unfamiliar with such a back-to-the-basics experience. Several local families, during the early 1960's and later, still saw indoor plumbing and running water as an expensive luxury. My grandmother's home was not equipped with indoor facilities until after her death in the mid-1970's.

The adventure came with the trip itself. If the need arose during cold weather months, the activity of getting unbundled in an "airish" (as the locals were fond of saying) environment was enough to encourage even the owners of the smallest kidneys to "wait just a little longer." Once erected, these outdoor shrines were not known for wonderful insulation.

In the summer months, the story was different. Making your way to the building was only half the challenge. Weeds, grass, dew and the tell-tale "beggar lice" could quickly sully those "Sunday go to meetin' clothes."

Once at the outhouse, still other challenges awaited. The structure seemed to be a magnet drawing all manner of creeping, slithering and flying life forms. Red wasps, dirt daubers, spiders, flies of the green and horse varieties, and the occasional chicken snake all served to keep visitors alert and attentive to their surroundings.

After making allowances for all of these issues, the time it took me to "do my business" that morning consumed a great portion of the preaching service. By the time Mom and I returned to our seats and settled in, it was almost time for the altar call and closing prayer. And Daddy hadn't said a word. Don't think I didn't notice.

During the week that followed, I created a plan. The next Sunday as the choir members retreated to their seats, I put my plan to the test.

"Mom."

"What is it, Phil?" she whispered.

"I gotta go."

"What?" she asked testily.

"I gotta go," I repeated.

"Are ya sure?"

"Yes, Ma'am," I replied, thinking proper manners appropriate in this situation.

Mom paused purposely and stared straight ahead. Finally, she drew a heavy breath. Obviously disgusted, she turned to me. "Well, come on. Mark, you might as well come, too," she said as we all crawled over Daddy to get to the aisle beyond.

As I passed in front of Daddy, I felt an eery sensation sweep over me. I sensed "the look." I didn't dare look up. I knew better. I just kept moving. As soon as we were safely in the aisle, well beyond his arm's reach, the uneasy feeling quickly passed. Seconds later we were merrily making our way down the now familiar path. My plan was working. By the time we returned, Brother Riley had completed his third sermon point and was barreling toward his closing poem and the altar call.

I was so proud. Later that afternoon, as Mark and I recapped, in private, the success of the past two outhouse odysseys, we determined that if the scam had worked so well the past two weeks, there was no reason to think a third time would be different. I had not yet realized the wisdom of Proverbs 16:18, "Pride goeth before destruction, and a haughty spirit before a fall." In my youthful exuberance and overconfidence, I had somehow totally disregarded Daddy.

The following Sunday morning rolled around quickly. As you might imagine, with the last few notes of "Amazing Grace" still lingering in the air, the imaginary urge struck.

"Mom. Mom!" I whispered loudly.

"What is it, Phil?"

"I gotta go out back," I responded with a new found level of confidence. I was already on my feet, anticipating our trip to the outhouse, when my well-laid plan began to crumble. Before Mom could respond, Daddy leaned forward, and to both mine and Mom's surprise, looked me coldly in the eye and said, "Come on boy. I'll take ya."

I was frozen in fear, but unfortunately, not in place. I felt Daddy's thick, calloused fingers wrap themselves around my skinny bicep. They closed quickly and tightly. Immediately, I felt myself being lifted, even propelled up and out of the pew and into the aisle. My feet waved helplessly in the air as Daddy took swift, determined steps that led us quickly through the back doors of the auditorium. On those few occasions when I was able to get one foot or the other to the floor, digging my heels into the worn scarlet colored carpet produced no results. I could hear myself saying, "Daddy, I changed my mind. I don't hafta go after all."

He simply looked down at me, head nodding vigorously, "the look" in full force.

"Oh, yeah, you're gonna go. I'm gonna make sure that ya go," he said, as we continued out of the building and down the path.

I will spare you additional details. I see no great benefit in recounting the rest of this particular experience. Let me simply state that there was no fear of a spared rod spoiling this child in Farmersville, Kentucky, on that Lord's day!

I often think of that experience and its value to me. As a child, I learned that disruptive, manipulative behavior would not, could not, be ignored or tolerated. I learned that the choices I make always have corresponding consequences. Some unpleasant. I also learned that when a person attempts to fool others, the person often becomes the fool.

One more thing. I still think twice and check over my shoulder before heading off to the restroom at church.

"Personally, I'm always ready to learn,
though I do not always like being taught."

WINSTON CHURCHILL

4

The Scarlet Letter

The sky was a beautiful shade of blue. Mockingbirds whistled cheerfully in the distance. Soft, sweet breezes blew. Springtime had finally arrived in western Kentucky. And I wasn't in the mood to enjoy any of it.

As I stood that afternoon, on the Caldwell County High School football field, my focus was not fixed on the sky, or birds or gentle breezes. More pressing issues occupied my mind.

First, spring football practice had just concluded for the day. As a fifteen year old, just finishing my freshman year of high school, I had been working diligently the past several weeks, hoping to attract the attention of the varsity coaching staff. More than anything else, I wanted to impress them during these spring practice sessions.

For years, I had dreamed of glorious Friday evenings spent on this field. Again and again, I had visualized myself pulling that blue and gold jersey over broad shoulder pads and then walking with silent determination toward this field of battle. I could easily envision myself joining other team members outside the stadium entrance as we waited with nervous anticipation for the signal to emerge. Then, at the precisely timed moment, we, the members of the Caldwell County Tigers varsity football squad, would spill through that stadium gate into this arena, this pit, where we would be greeted by cheering fans and marching bands and the general fanfare that accompanied small town high school football.

This was my dream. I could see it. I could hear it. I could even feel it. It was finally within reach. But, first I had to make the team. To make the team, I had to make an impression.

It was not unheard of to have an incoming sophomore play

a key role on the varsity squad. But, it was not easy either. Besides the obvious need for appropriate size and talent, I had already determined that attitude seemed to be a major determining factor in the decisions the coaches made. Thus, I believed that what I couldn't control relative to size, talent and experience, I could more than make up for in desire, hustle and aggressiveness. I wanted the coaching staff to recognize my level of commitment. I wanted them to see, firsthand, that I was willing to do the work that was required.

My second pressing issue of the day involved academics not athletics. I don't want to give the misguided impression that I was a poor student. I wasn't. I had always done well in school. Throughout the years, I had been one of those students for whom schoolwork had basically been a breeze. It came easy for me. I had crafted, refined and applied a study plan that had resulted in repeated classroom success. My recipe was simple:

Don't skip too many classes;
try to pay attention when you're there;
take pretty good notes;
do most of the homework; and
glance over your notes before the tests.

This self-styled approach had served me well. It proved good enough to routinely earn me A's, with an occasional B mixed in for good measure. Oh, sure, I *could* have worked harder and probably made all A's. But, my past successes had lulled me into a very comfortable zone. In fact, I had discovered how to be intellectually lazy and still achieve some measure of academic success.

However, during my freshman year of high school, I had encountered a few more academic challenges. First of all, the curriculums were more demanding than I had initially expected. Not overwhelming, just more demanding. My almost immediate response to this new found realization? Simple. I adapted, fine tuned if you will, my earlier recipe for classroom success:

Skip <u>fewer</u> classes;
pay <u>closer</u> attention;
take <u>better</u> notes;
<u>do</u> the homework; and
<u>review</u> the notes <u>more</u> <u>carefully</u> before tests.

My second challenge and the one that I had not yet mastered involved project work. I'm referring to those frustrating assignments that required work outside the classroom. Term papers and book reports proved to be the most irritating thorns in my side. I firmly believed that schoolwork ought to be restricted to school. How dare those thoughtless educators assign work that would cut into my social time and extracurricular activities! I don't care if they did give me sixteen weeks prior notice to complete a specific project. It's simply too much to ask of any normal, red blooded student! Or so I thought.

With those types of thoughts drifting in and out of my mind, there I stood on the forty yard line, suffering equally from the lingering effects of wind sprints and a self induced, overblown case of the "it's just not fair's." Not recognizing my psychological dilemma or current state of mind, my buddy, Jim McDaniel stood doubled over several yards away, still trying to catch his breath.

"Hey, man," began McDaniel, almost spitting out the words between labored breaths. "Whatcha doin' tonight?"

Still attempting to recover from the last grueling wind sprint, I recognized immediately who Jim was talking to. But, I didn't feel like talking. Not to him, not to anybody. I chose not to respond.

"Hey, Fuzzy!" McDaniel asserted louder, this time using his favorite nickname for me.

At that time, Jim McDaniel was a relatively new friend. Two years earlier, during seventh grade, Jim's family had moved back to Princeton, from Detroit. I learned that his mom and dad were natives of the area who, years earlier, had moved north in search of job opportunities. However, after their children came along, Wanda and Roy McDaniel decided to return to Kentucky to raise their kids in a more familiar environment.

It's probably important to note that a common activity at that time was the assignment of nicknames. Almost every guy I knew had one and even some of the girls. Often they were simply a derivative of the individual's name, such as "A.J." for Anna Jo, "Stal" for Stallins, "Big Al" for Alan, "Murph" for Murphy, "Augie" for Alsobrook and so on. Other nicknames seemed to catch on because of their more descriptive nature. Some were quite colorful. Tank, Rooster, Mighty Mouse, Rock, Hoss, Runt, Bluegill, Wildman, Bird Legs, Wookie, Skeeter, Snake and Hot Dog were some of the more memorable. For some, these monikers were enjoyed and promoted, while for others they were detested. Most were simply tolerated. Why? Because the more one fought to become disassociated with an unflattering nickname, the more it seemed to stick.

Jim's nickname was harmless enough. His father's name was Roy. Since he and his father resembled each other in appearance and stature, he naturally became "Little Roy" or just "Roy." Everybody liked Jim's dad, so Jim wore his nickname proudly.

That was not necessarily the case with me. I earned my nickname because I began to physically mature a little earlier than most of my male counterparts. During fifth and sixth grades, I began to have noticeable growth of body hair—legs, arms, chest and so on. During seventh grade, it became necessary for me to begin shaving my face. I was one of the first, if not *the* first, boy in my class to do so. As a result, what began as good natured teasing: "Van Hooser, shave that peach fuzz!" was soon shortened to "Fuzzy" or "Fuzz." A nickname was born.

"Fuzz, I'm talkin' to you!"

"What?" I replied testily.

"Hey, buddy, what's got your shorts in a wad?" McDaniel responded sarcastically.

"Nothin'," I said, downplaying his sarcasm. "Whatta ya want?"

"I was just wonderin' whatcha gonna be doin' tonight."

"Readin'," I replied with obvious disgust.

"Readin'? Readin' what?"

"Oh, I gotta oral book report due in Miss Tandy's Literature class day after tomorrow and I haven't finished readin' the book yet."

"What book is it?" McDaniel asked.

"The Scarlet Letter, by Nathaniel Hawthorne."

"Never heard of it," McDaniel replied. "What's it about?"

"How should I know? I told you I haven't read it."

"Ya mean ya haven't read *any* of it? When did she assign it anyway?"

"Oh, she assigned it the first week of the semester. She gave each person in class a novel to read. She told us that our main grade would come from the oral reports that we did on the book at the end of the semester. I started on it several weeks ago. But, I swear, I couldn't get past the first thirty pages. It is dry as dirt! Now, I got about two hundred pages to read and a report to prepare in less than two days. Man, I'm outta time. I don't know what I'm gonna do."

"Have ya checked about *Cliffs Notes* for it?" the always pragmatic McDaniel asked, trying to be helpful.

"Of course I checked. I can't find any anywhere," I replied.

While McDaniel and I talked, most of the other players drifted off the field, headed for the dressing room and a hot shower. The field was almost deserted. As I glanced around, I noticed one of the coaches walking toward us. It was Charlie Davis.

Coach Davis was a junior high science teacher during the day and a football coach once classes were through. He was the one coach on the entire staff that I knew best. Not that I was one of his favorites, or anything like that. It's just that I had been in his science class a couple of years earlier and had played for him on both the seventh and eighth grade football teams. I genuinely liked him, despite his fondness for sarcasm.

"Girls, what seems to be the problem?" Coach Davis asked

as he approached. "Are ya hurt?"

"No, sir," we both replied, trying to ignore the insult to our budding masculinity.

"Then why are ya still out here? Do ya have a problem?"

"Van Hooser does," McDaniel replied with a chuckle.

I gave McDaniel my coldest stare.

"Well, Little Roy, what's Van Hooser's problem?"

By this time, Jim had recognized the full effect of my stare.

"Oh, I'll let him tell ya. I gotta catch a ride." With those words, Jim began jogging toward the gate that led to the dressing room. I was left standing with Coach Davis. He turned his full attention to me.

"Mr. Van Hooser, do ya have a problem?" Coach Davis asked directly.

"Well, a little one."

"Would ya like to share it with me? Maybe I can be of some help."

I listened to his words and studied his body language carefully, searching for any evidence of either sarcasm or sincerity. Neither was quickly apparent. In the absence of identified sarcasm, I assumed he was sincerely interested. Maybe he could help me out. At this point, I was desperate.

"Well, it's like this. I've got a book report due day after tomorrow and I haven't *quite* finished the book yet. Coach, I've been so busy with tests and football practice and everything else that I just haven't been able to finish it all," I said, with a manufactured hint of pain in my voice, which I hoped would evoke some sympathy.

Even though I felt a slight tinge of guilt by giving the impression that I had read most of the book, at that moment, a little white lie seemed safer than telling the unadulterated truth. After all, Coach Davis was still a teacher. He might be inclined to side with Miss Tandy on this one. The coach just looked at me.

"What book?" he asked.

"The Scarlet Letter," I replied.

Coach Davis just nodded and looked away for a moment.

"Got any suggestions?" I asked meekly.

He returned his gaze and focused it directly on me.

"Maybe," he began.

I was immediately optimistic. My hope grew.

"I'm very familiar with the book, Phil. I've read it several times in the past for different classes myself. First, let me ask ya, exactly how much of it have ya read?"

His question nailed me. This is where the crystal clear distinction between right and wrong blurred significantly for me. I had already led him to believe that I had read quite a bit of the book. Should I fess up and come clean now, or continue my bluff. I looked him straight in the eye. I was in too deep.

"Almost all of it," I lied, with as much feigned sincerity as I could muster. "I just haven't been able to finish it."

A slight, fleeting smile passed his lips.

"In that case, ya already know that the story unfolds during the eighteenth century in puritanical Massachusetts," he offered, sounding very certain of himself. Very official. "I'm sure ya remember that the story focuses on the act of adultery and sets about to explore the personal and societal implications of the sinful action."

"It does?" I thought. "I don't remember any of that in the first thirty pages. Maybe I shoulda stuck with it after all. Sounds interesting. Too late for that now. Just pay close attention and make good mental notes."

Coach Davis didn't demand a response from me. He continued very formally. "Mr. Van Hooser, there are three things that ya need to be sure to discuss during your oral report. Keep in mind that the primary character, Hester Prynne, has an illicit, adulterous affair which produces an illegitimate child. When she refuses to publicly identify the father of the child, the local judiciary, with encouragement from the townspeople, decides to both humiliate her personally and to use her as a public example. Therefore, her punishment required her to wear the sewn scarlet letter 'A', signifying 'adulteress', on all her garments. As a result, all she met would be aware of her indiscretion. Phil, ya do remember this don't ya?"

"Yes, sir," I said, as I tried desperately to keep the details straight in my mind. "Is there anything else ya think I should include in my report?"

Coach Davis looked at me and smiled broadly. Soon his smile faded, he became very serious.

"Phil," Coach Davis said very solemnly, "the two key elements of the rest of the book center around the child and the father of the child, whose identity remained unknown to the residents of the community. For the sake of your report, it's *critical* that you acknowledge the child's name, *Primrose,* and the occupation of the illegitimate child's father, *a traveling salesman.*"

What great details! I was certain that I could weave them into an acceptable report. I could hardly wait to get started. I thanked the coach profusely for his help, as I hurried for the locker room.

I was the third presenter of the morning. The first two presenters shared in-depth reports on very forgettable books. As they worked hard to share their unique insights and literary analysis, gleaned from careful reading and study during the past fourteen weeks, I glanced around the class at the other students. As could be predicted, some were listening dutifully, even taking notes. Most, however, were engaged in other various activities designed to make the hour go more quickly and painlessly. Some doodled on lined spiral notebook paper spread out in front of them. Others were deeply involved in passing critical messages, in the form of notes, to fellow classmates. Some, like me, squirmed nervously in their seats, anticipating their upcoming presentation. Finally, a few of the more obviously unmotivated students sat motionless, with heads buried deep in crossed arms that rested on their desk's surface. During occasional momentary breaks in the presentations, if one listened closely, occasionally deep, ragged breaths, emitted by the napper, could be heard. These always brought muffled giggles throughout the room.

I also kept a close eye on Miss Tandy. Miss Tandy was young, as compared to almost all my other teachers. In her mid to late twenties, she was not long removed from her own formal educational pursuits. She was attractive and composed. Though young and relatively inexperienced, she was still able to create an air of authority and respect without seeming overbearing. Her professionalism translated into overall classroom control. I liked her.

After the announcements and instructions for the day had been given, Miss Tandy had positioned herself at the back of the room. From that vantage point, she listened intently to each presentation, while still closely monitoring the behavior of those students not presenting. As the presentations unfolded, she would quietly make notes, which would apparently be used later for her formal evaluation of each presentation. Once each presentation was concluded, Miss Tandy would applaud politely, thank each presenter for their efforts and then call for the next presentation to begin.

"My book report is on *The Scarlet Letter*," I began boldly. "It's an important book that focuses on a publicly ostracized woman who was made to wear a scarlet letter after bearing an illegitimate daughter, Primrose, following a secretive romance with a traveling salesman."

One by one, my classmates began to sit noticeably straighter. Many responded with what could be best described as rapt attention. Even the nappers, interrupted by the change of speakers, struggled to fight off sleep for just a few minutes longer. I was certain that none had read this book, and they were obviously finding the titillating theme to be as engaging as I did, when Coach Davis shared it with me two days earlier. But, without question, the most attentive person in the room was none other than Miss Tandy. Throughout my brief presentation, she never took a note. Her eyes never left me. She sat ramrod straight, her piercing stare trained directly on my eyes.

After stumbling along for two or three more uncertain minutes, I finally found my way to my prepared, albeit generic, close. My concluding comments went something like this, "I highly recommend that each of ya take the time to read this book. If ya do, I'm sure you'll find it to be as interesting and thought provoking as I did. Thanks."

With a smattering of applause echoing through the room, I thankfully began to make my way back to my seat. Before I was successful, I heard the following words.

"Excuse me, Phillip. Before you sit down, I would like to ask you a few questions." The voice belonged to Miss Tandy, but it was the word 'Phillip' that stopped me dead in my tracks. Almost everybody called me 'Phil.' Everybody, that is, except my mom when she had caught me in the act of doing something that I shouldn't. The sensation was unmistakable.

"Phillip, *The Scarlet Letter* is one of my favorite books," she reported evenly.

How could I be so stupid! Not once had I considered the fact that maybe she had actually *read* this book! I had assumed that all teachers head off to the library, snatch the first books they come to off the shelves, and then assign them to students at random. This was not good!

"If I am not mistaken, I believe I heard you say that the child in this book was named *Primrose*. Is that correct?"

"Yes, ma'am," I responded meekly.

"I seem to recall that the child's name was *Pearl,*" she said, without requesting a response. It was a good thing a response was not requested, because I would never have been able to offer one. I couldn't speak. I could barely breathe. I just stood staring blankly at her. She went on.

"Phillip, I also distinctly remember that the father of this illegitimate child was the local *minister,* not a *traveling salesman* as you suggested. His elevated position and stature in the community added to the scandalous nature of the offense."

By this point, I was absolutely frozen in fear. I had been found out by Miss Tandy, and now my peers were beginning to catch on, too.

"Phillip, one final question. Did you even read this book?"

Somewhere deep in the recesses of my mind, I heard those ageless words, with the timeless message, return to me, "Be sure, your sins will find you out," followed closely by, "Oh, what a tangled web we weave, when first we practice to deceive." I finally had to come clean. In the end, Miss Tandy was much more generous with my grade than she should have been. But the lesson that I learned was much more valuable to me than any that might have come from the pages of Hawthorne's *The Scarlet Letter.*

Thank goodness for the Miss Tandys of the world.

One other thing. You can find me sitting in the back row of the 1972 Caldwell County Tigers varsity football team picture. I'm the one wearing the scarlet letter "G." It stands for "gullible."

Thanks, Coach.

---

*"Teachers can change lives with just
the right mix of chalk and challenges."*
JOYCE A. MYERS

Learnin' How

"Learning is remembering what you're interested in. That's pretty close to entertainment."

RICHARD SAUL WURMAN

- **Hog Heaven**
- **King of the Slab**
- **Battle Scars**
- **Uncle Harvey**

5

Hog Heaven

Don't ask me why, but I have always had an affinity for pigs. I have often heard Mom tell that while I was just a toddler, she caught me scribbling enthusiastically on one of the walls of our home with a crayon. When asked what I was doing, I reported proudly that I was drawing pigs. As I think back on it now, a more apt description might be that they were drawing me. Irresistibly drawing me to them.

My first crack at entrepreneurialism occurred when I was about fourteen years old. My parents had bought a rundown farm in the section of Caldwell County that natives referred to as the Briarfield community. As it turned out, that name proved to be an appropriate description of our new farm. A briar field! Exactly the challenge that my dad had in mind for his two oldest boys as they rapidly approached adolescence and ultimately, young adulthood.

Not that he communicated his plans exactly that way. He phrased it much more simply. "Since Phil and Mark have all this new found energy, it's high time they learned how to work."

Having been a product of an agricultural environment himself, Daddy became convinced that buying a rundown, overgrown farm was a wonderful idea. From his perspective, there was simply no better locale to shape the mind, muscles and manner of his sons. He saw this project to be a great proving ground leading to impending manhood.

As I look back on the experience today, I can't argue with his logic at all. But, I must admit, that while teetering on the brink of becoming a man, I had serious questions concerning his line of reasoning. Instead of every spare minute being spent clearing ground, building fences and hauling rocks out of the fields, my young mind was drifting more to thoughts of ball games, leisurely afternoons at the lake, and of course, girls. However, I never remember Daddy asking for my opinion. Frankly, I'm sure he didn't. For him, there were lessons to be taught and work to be done. The farm would be a wonderful classroom. Soon, our education was under way.

Not long after the ink had dried on the deed to our new farm, we found ourselves wading armpit deep through briars and brambles, thorns and thistles, honeysuckles and horse-weeds, just to see if a farm actually existed. We quickly learned that the chainsaw and grubbing hoe would have to wait. Daddy hired a bulldozer and operator to jumpstart this land reclamation process. I also learned quickly that a few hours of dozer work can produce weeks of backbreaking, follow up labor for "the boys." Picking up roots, cutting firewood, building and burning brush piles and removing dislodged field rock would be a brief, but accurate description of our physical activities for the next several months.

As the initial clearing work progressed, Daddy turned his attention to what I would discover was his next favorite farming activity—fence building.

For one of my early grade school assignments, I distinctly remember my teacher instructing each class member to go home that afternoon and get our fathers to give us his favorite quotation and his autograph. These many years later, it would be fruitless to ask me to quote the Gettysburg address, the pre-amble to the Constitution, or any of the French dialogue, which I may have learned at some point. However, without hesitation, I can still recite precisely the quote that my dad offered:

*"Anything worth doing
is worth doing right."*

I'm sure the quote can be traced and attributed to some great historic figure. That doesn't matter to me. The quote was as much Daddy's as whoever first spoke or penned the words.

Why? Because long ago, he had internalized its message, concept and scope. It was simple, straightforward, solid. It was also his view on life and work. As this principle related to the activity of fence building, I soon learned that he intended to practice what he preached.

As we began construction on one of our first stretches of fence, I realized that Daddy had determined that this was one of those jobs that "...is worth doing right." He handpicked every cedar post to be used. Each was of virtually the same size and quality. Individual postholes were dug by hand. The depth of each was to be twenty-four inches, give or take a fraction of an inch. After dropping each post into the freshly dug holes, we were instructed to bear-hug, man handle and eventually position each and every post in such a way as to assure that the smoothest side always faced the road.

Once all the posts were positioned appropriately in the ground, the real work began. All corner and brace posts were set in concrete. At that time, we knew nothing of ready mixed concrete. The concrete we used was mixed by hand, on site. Two and a half shovels full of gravel, mixed with an equal amount of lime and one portion of dry concrete mix. Add water. Not too much water. The mixture should be sticky, not soupy. Thorough mixing of this concrete concoction was accomplished by repeatedly pouring the contents, back and forth, from one five-gallon bucket into a second, empty bucket. This backbreaking manual mixing procedure continued, bucket to bucket, until all the dry particles were thoroughly moistened. Always remembering—sticky, not soupy!

Next, the mixture would be poured into hole after hole, each containing an individual cedar post. The process was basically a three-man operation. One man to position and hold the posts in a perfectly perpendicular manner—smooth side still facing the road. A second man to gradually fill the hollowed out void surrounding the posts with the concrete mixture. Finally, a third man to "tamp" the concrete mixture down into the hole with a "tamping stick." Tamping sticks were commonly made from a steel rebar rod or a sturdy sassafras sapling, about five to six feet in length. This tamping activity was critical to ensure that no air pockets remained between the moist concrete and the post, which might later allow the post, and ultimately, the fence, to shift, sag or lean.

For those posts not of the corner or brace variety, the process differed slightly. Generally, these "line" posts were not set in concrete. The use of concrete was determined to be unnecessary for line posts, because the pressure on them was significantly less than that of their corner and brace post cousins. However, the tamping process remained ever important. In place of concrete, Daddy would have us use straight gravel and field rock, mixed with dirt to strengthen and fortify the posts foundation. For him, tamping with mere dirt was never enough. He knew that over time, the dirt in the postholes would settle, thereby allowing the post to loosen itself from its mooring. Once wire was attached to the individual posts, if they had not been solidly placed and secured, the pressure from the tautly strung wire could eventually dislodge them from their holes. It's hard to get livestock to take seriously a fence whose posts spend their days dangling in the wind.

The result of the first phase of the fence building process was a line of rigid cedar soldiers, standing straight and tall, in perfect formation, along the road. They stood patiently awaiting their metallic adornment. The adornment would soon come.

When the concrete moorings had set and hardened for twenty-four hours or so, phase two of the fence building process was ready to begin. The wire intended to complete the fence would be unloaded and positioned close to the waiting corner posts. The end of the wire would be firmly attached to a corner post and would then be unrolled along side the other standing posts. When a significant portion of the wire had been unrolled, we had to stretch it tightly and nail it securely to the posts.

If the area being fenced was intended to contain only cattle, then the traditional wire of choice was "barbed wire." (Commonly known throughout western Kentucky as "bob ware.") If, on the other hand, the field being fenced was to be a multipurpose one (cattle, hogs, or goats) "woven wire" would be selected. If barbed wire was chosen, at least four strands, occasionally five, would be positioned, equal distance, up and down the posts. For woven wire, Daddy still believed in putting a couple of strands of barbed wire above the woven wire. It was his way of not so gently dissuading cattle from putting their heads over the fence and simply using the weight and pressure from their necks and shoulders to eventually break the fence down.

From Daddy's view point, it was absolutely necessary that the process be a meticulous one, with little margin for error. No shortcuts were allowed or tolerated. The result? Joe Van Hooser fences rated high on both appearance and functionality. Today I can report that fences we constructed more than a quarter century ago are still serving their productive purposes. Simply put, in keeping with Joe Van Hooser's philosophy and under his direction "...we did it right!"

One evening, after supper and a long day of fence building, Daddy summoned Mark and me into the dining room. From the outset, this conversation appeared unusual. The tone of his voice was different.

"Pull up a chair boys. I've gotta business proposition to discuss with ya."

His manner seemed upbeat and direct. Nevertheless, I was apprehensive. I looked him over carefully. He was clean-shaven, with his graying hair neatly combed up and over in his lifelong style. Seated in his customary position at the head of the table, he wore an aging, thread bare, sleeveless T-shirt. The work pants he had on were clean, but also well worn. His bare feet poked out of the cuffed pant legs. His work boots sat along the wall nearby as if waiting to be called to duty at any moment.

Spread out in front of Daddy sat a half full cup of Maxwell

House instant coffee, a cheap ball point pen, (no doubt an intended enticement from some long forgotten local political candidate), and a previously discarded envelope which he had apparently salvaged from the trash can. On the back of the envelope were all the telltale signs. No doubt about it. He had been "figurin'."

Across the serving bar from where Daddy sat, Mom stood quietly at the kitchen sink, still working to restore order following the evening meal. As she washed and dried a seemingly endless array of pots, pans and plates, her primary attention remained keenly fixed on the scene playing out around her. It was plain to see that she knew what was going on. She was in on it.

"Boys," my dad began. "Y'all know that we've been puttin' a lot of time, money and effort into fixin' up that old farm. Y'all can also tell that it's finally beginnin' to shape up some. I'm wonderin' if you're interested in joinin' me in a three-way partnership deal to make a little money?"

Neither of us spoke.

Interested? Sure we were interested in making a little money. But, we were plowing new ground here. Never before had we been in a partnership with him, or anyone else for that matter, on anything. We had absolutely no past precedent or experience to draw from. We just sat in silence. Looking and feeling confused.

"Well, are ya interested or not?" he insisted.

"Well, I guess," we responded. "But doin' what?"

Quickly, he began to lay out his plan.

"Since we finally have some fence built, I think it's time we look into gettin' some livestock. How'd y'all like to get in the hog business?"

The hog business? I had never even entertained the thought. I liked hogs. I always had. And, making money sounded very appealing to me. But, as I recalled his earlier words, I distinctly remembered him saying something about a three-way partnership. I thought it took money to form a partnership. If so, that would be a major sticking point for me. I just didn't have any. Not many fourteen year olds, that I knew, did.

"How much'll it cost?" I asked, trying to sound grown up.

Daddy just grinned.

"Well, this is the way I got it figured," he said, as he turned his full attention to his business plan, otherwise known as the envelope.

"Up to now, I've furnished all the materials for the fencin' and y'all have furnished most of the labor. And I haven't paid ya anything."

I was glad he chose not to overlook that specific detail.

"All we need now to get started is to build some kinda hog house, buy a feeder and get some hogs. Here's my deal. I'll furnish the materials for the hog house and we'll build it together. And I'll buy the hog feeder and the first load of feed. Then y'all will be responsible for buying the hogs and for takin' care of 'em. After the first load, we'll split the cost of the feed three ways. When it's time to take the hogs to market, we'll split the check three ways. How's it sound?"

My mind was racing. It sounded great, except for two things. How much would the hogs cost? And how many would we buy? I had no idea. I had to ask.

"It sounds fair," I said evenly, trying to sound more mature than my fourteen years would allow. "But, how many hogs will we need and how much will they run us?"

"I've already talked to Paul Watson and he has two gilts that he'll sell y'all. One is a Hampshire (black with a white band around its shoulder area) and the other is a Yorkshire (solid white with upright ears). Both of 'em are due to pig in the next few weeks. Paul wants a hundred and fifty dollars for both."

Paul Watson was a fair man. He and his wife, Margie—Puddin' as he called her—had been a part of our lives for as far back as I could remember. Paul, Margie, Mom and Dad were best friends. Paul and Daddy had worked together on several projects in the past. They were as close as brothers. As a result,

I considered him to be an uncle, without the blood connection. I knew Paul Watson would never take advantage of us. But, a hundred and fifty dollars?! That amounted to a sizable fortune for us. Even though I didn't recognize it at the time, we were encountering our first entrepreneurial obstacle. Financing.

"Daddy, let us check how much we got." With those words, Mark and I adjourned to another room to conduct a hasty financial audit.

Just as I am unable to explain how Jesus was able to feed five thousand souls with nothing more than five loaves and two fishes, I am unable to explain how Mark and I were able to scrape up one hundred and fifty dollars to buy those gilts. Maybe we had it in our savings. Maybe we sold something. Maybe Mom intervened. To this day, I'm still not sure how we secured the money. That particular detail simply evades me. But, somehow, between the two of us, we were able to scrape up the required cash and the deal was struck.

Over the next few days, all the necessary details were attended to. Purchase arrangements were made and delivery taken on our newly created swine herd. Both of them. Just like that, we were in the hog business. It was a very exciting time. We eagerly set about tending to our burgeoning livestock empire.

The Yorkshire gilt was the first to deliver. Just a few short weeks after being purchased, she delivered nine of the finest pigs I had ever seen. We were thrilled. Overjoyed. Mark and I immediately, although prematurely, began to count the money we were certain we would receive from the eventual sale of these newborn piglets. We quickly convinced ourselves that fame—or at least fortune—would soon be ours. Pork barons before we were old enough to drive! Move over Jimmy Dean. Life was good. We were truly experiencing "hog heaven."

Unfortunately, the reality of life proved less kind than our youthful imaginations. Porcine tragedy struck.

A short time after the arrival of the first litter, it came time for gilt number two to give birth. Tragically, while delivering her litter, the Hampshire gilt suffered serious complications. She and all her pigs were lost.

We were devastated. I had learned much earlier about the facts of life and death on the farm. I understood that farm animals were commodities, not pets. It was fine to enjoy them in the moment, but when the time came to cart them off to market, no tears were to be shed. None were.

But, this was different. We had such high hopes. We had so much of ourselves invested in this venture.

My thoughts were admittedly self-centered. In a matter of minutes, we watched helplessly as one half of our business investment disappeared. In a very real sense, a significant portion of my youthful innocence died with that gilt and her young. I was learning some of the rudimentary rules of entrepreneurism: don't count your pigs before they're weaned, fortunes are elusive, and setbacks happen.

A few mornings after we had suffered that first devastating setback, Paul Watson made an unexpected visit to our house.

"Boys, I heard about ya losin' that gilt this week. I want ya to know how bad I feel about the whole thing."

His words were thoughtful and honest. "I feel bad that I didn't recognize that somethin' was wrong with her. I woulda never sold her to ya if I'd a suspected anything might be wrong."

Again, we believed him. How could he have known? There was no way.

"Anyway, I wanna make it up to y'all."

Suddenly, my ears perked up. My downcast disposition started to brighten somewhat.

"I'll be happy to either give ya back the seventy-five dollars that ya paid for her, or I'll replace her with another gilt. Your choice."

Oh, happy day! I was thrilled. What a guy!

Personally, I immediately began to lean toward the cash refund as the better of the two options. Over the past few days, during the height of my personal pity party, I had come to the basic conclusion that my future wasn't in pork bellies after all. But, before the discussion proceeded any farther, Daddy interceded.

"Thanks, Paul, but the boys won't be takin' ya up on either offer. Will ya boys?"

His question was constructed and delivered in such a manner that there was no mistaking the correct answer.

"No, thanks, Paul," we both mumbled unenthusiastically, with heads hung low.

So ended the conversation.

Now, almost three decades later, I think I better appreciate the lessons learned from that experience. Through it, I learned that personal and professional optimism is always best when tempered with a healthy dose of realism.

I learned something else of even more value. I learned that some people love you so much, they are willing to bail you out of your problems. And some people love you so much, they won't.

Each one a lesson from heaven.

Hog heaven.

———

*"No man should be allowed to be president
who doesn't understand hogs."*

HARRY S. TRUMAN

6

King of the Slab

During the summer between my sophomore and junior years in high school, I landed my first "real job." I stress real job, because prior to it, all I had done was "work." The work to which I'm referring was work in its truest sense. Taxing, unglamorous, physical labor. Not some enjoyable, leisurely, comfortable activity for which I was paid a salary. I was envious of many of my friends who had secured summer jobs as lifeguards, store clerks, baseball grounds keepers, or interns at one of the nearby Kentucky State Parks.

You see, my year round labors had been confined to the family farm—putting out crops, working with livestock, raising tobacco, hauling hay, clearing ground, building fences, harvesting crops and then starting the process all over again. The cycle was endless. General farm labor. For such work, I received no hourly compensation. My compensation, infrequent as it was, came once the tobacco crop sold in the winter or after the hogs were carted off to market in the spring.

As the months of my adolescence passed, things began to change for me. More specifically, I began to change. I matured physically. In a relatively short period of time, there was a noticeable increase in my size, strength and stamina. Noticeable to me, but also noticeable to others. Because farming activities at that time were still very labor intensive, size, strength and stamina were valuable assets. A "strong back and weak mind" were in great demand.

My blossoming physical potential, coupled with my farming background, made me an attractive commodity with other area farmers. Farmers who found themselves with more work to do than sons or sons-in-law to do it. Farmers who sporadically needed help disking fields, hauling hay or setting out and later in the year, harvesting tobacco crops. There was never a shortage of farm work for me to do. My problem was that I wanted, I needed, more variety.

Another significant change took place about the same time. I was awarded my driver's license. Seemingly overnight I achieved the mobility every sixteen year old longs for. I was certain that personal independence and adventure could not be far behind. Unfortunately, I quickly learned that a driver's license and mobility meant very little with no gas money to fuel this new found independence.

Oh, I found many creative and shallow attempts to overcome this financial instability. Many post football practice gatherings found me huddled once again with my "runnin' buddies" McDaniel, Stallins or Tompkins. This time not for the purpose of creating some defensive strategy designed to stop our opponent. Instead, we were continuously engaged in pooling our meager resources to finance that evening's entertainment, which more often than not involved circling "The Queen."

The local Burger Queen restaurant was the mecca of youth socialization in Princeton, Kentucky. It was the place to see and be seen in our little town of seven thousand five hundred people. Many school lunches were skipped, returnable Coke bottles sold, and meager savings accounts pilfered in an effort to provide some personal contribution to this worthy cause. As we frequently reminded one another, sacrificial giving was the key.

Unfortunately, our sparse resources frequently proved woefully insufficient to fund our independence and sense of adventure. The time had come to take more drastic action. I was motivated. It was time for me to get a "real job." One with established hours, a set wage and a regular check at the end of each week. Of course, it wouldn't hurt if there was a little more glamour to it than working on the farm.

For me, my options were limited. I have never been

mechanically inclined. I knew next to nothing about cars. Therefore, pumping gas at some full service gas station (in the days before they became extinct) was not a viable option for me.

I owned a couple pair of faded blue jeans, but no white shirt or skinny black tie. Therefore, the ever-available grocery store "carry out" position was also out of the question.

After a period of diligent searching, I finally realized I needed to fall back on what I knew. For me, the only viable option was to explore possible openings at the "Experiment Farm."

The University of Kentucky Agricultural Research Farm and Experiment Station was its official name. But, around town it was simply known as the "Experiment Farm." The Experiment Farm was one of two or three such state owned facilities operated by the College of Agriculture at the University of Kentucky. The Princeton facility was located about two miles southeast of the courthouse square. It was nestled between the Sandlick Road to the east and the Hoptown (Hopkinsville for the uninitiated) Road to the south.

It was a local showplace. Twelve hundred acres of hills, woods, pastures, ponds, orchards, experimental plots, woven wire and white plank fences, livestock, manicured fields and well kept barns and buildings. It was the site of on-going agricultural research and experimentation designed to assist the farmers and landowners of western Kentucky and beyond. Designated departments within the Experiment Farm's structure studied issues involving tobacco, horticulture, agronomy, entomology and animal science. Each of these departments hired a few students each summer to help with the required tasks related to specific projects. In addition, several other students were hired each summer for the necessary, but less glamorous tasks known as "general farm maintenance." This job category involved the more routine activities of tractor driving, mowing, fruit gathering, hay hauling, fence and barn painting and so on.

I was desperate. I needed a job. Any job that was regular

and somewhat profitable. The Experiment Farm seemed to be my best option considering my limited marketable skills.

I relentlessly began calling and begging for an opportunity to "talk to someone about a job." After several weeks of persistent telephone calls and uninvited visits, I was finally granted my first official job interview, such as it was. Think about it. What probing questions can you ask a sixteen year old high school sophomore with virtually no work history or experience?

"Phil, what do you see yourself doing in ten years?"

"Uh, I don't really know yet."

"Okay then, what kind of job would you like to have here?"

"I'll take anything," was my predictable reply.

"Well, why do you want this job?"

"I really need to make some money."

"Oh, I see, Phil. You are money motivated. Are you saving for a car or for college?"

"Well, neither really. See, I'd really like to get a girlfriend some of these days."

Even I could tell the interview was not going well. I was confident that my interviewer had not stumbled upon any compelling reason to offer me one of his precious, much sought after summer jobs. More than anything else, I sensed that he was trying to get through the interview so that I wouldn't continue to worry him in the future. But, even in the darkest of hours, a glimmer of hope can shine through. Or said a different way, blind hogs do find an acorn every now and then.

In apparent desperation, the farm manager finally asked, "Phil, why should I hire you?"

Finally, a question I understood. A question I had thought about. A question I felt confident I could answer.

"Sir, I know how to work. I'm not afraid of work. I work on our family farm now. I also work for other farmers in the area when they need help. Right now, my dad, my brother and me are in partnership on some hogs that we own. I just know that if ya hire me ya won't be sorry."

Simple, honest and to the point. Somehow, I sensed my answer struck a responsive cord with my interviewer. A few weeks later, I learned I had landed my first real job. I was to start on the Monday after school let out for the summer. My specific job assignment would be announced then. I was thrilled!

Nervously, I checked my watch as I stepped out of the car in the Experiment Farm parking lot. 7:15 a.m. Good, fifteen minutes early. As I rechecked my directions and began the deliberate, anxious walk toward the room where I was to report, I mentally reviewed the coaching my parents had offered over breakfast: *get there early...stand up straight...do what you're told...say "yes sir" and "no sir"...listen...don't drag around...do your best...be quick to offer your help...work hard...show your appreciation...remember who you are...*and so on.

As I stepped through the door labeled "Break Room," I immediately noticed a momentary, yet distinctive hush. Every head turned in my direction. I paused. Few faces were familiar to me. Besides myself, several other guys from school had landed one of these coveted summertime positions. I quickly found the half dozen or so of them standing awkwardly together, speaking in hushed tones, at the far end of the room. Their attempts to be inconspicuous were obviously unsuccessful. I was certain that they had received the same treatment, upon entering, as I had.

Unfamiliar faces far outnumbered the familiar ones. Scattered throughout the room, smoking, eating, reading and drinking coffee were men, of various ages, sizes and skin colors. The permanent, fulltime employees were easily identified. Not only did they occupy the best seats in the room, they were noticeably older. Ranging in age from the mid twenties to fifty or better, these year round employees sported standard uniforms. Navy blue cotton twill pants and gray short sleeved shirts with names emblazoned over their hearts. William, Gary,

Bobby, Royce, Mark, Junior, Gayle Lee and so on, they read. I quickly noticed various reactions from this group toward me, upon my entry. Several stopped what they were doing entirely and looked me up and down. Others glanced my way briefly, before returning to their newspapers. One individual, from a card playing foursome, glanced back over his shoulder at me. Having quickly, but to his satisfaction, sufficiently sized me up, he turned his attention once again to his playing partners, while loudly proclaiming, "More fresh meat." His comment was punctuated with laughter. Initially his own, but soon joined by others. This wasn't quite the warm, open armed greeting I had hoped for in my first real job.

"Welcome to the work world," I thought.

As I crossed the threshold and entered the room, I nodded meekly to those who seemed remotely interested. To no one in particular, I mumbled a less than convincing, "Good mornin'." Quickly, I moved to join my peers at the far end of the room. During the uncomfortable minutes that followed, more individuals entered the room. Variations of the previous scene were played out until, at precisely 7:30 a.m., the door to the break room swung open and through it walked three men in standard farm uniform. Leading them was a younger man wearing a crisply starched white shirt and tie. His appearance and dress stood in stark contrast to the rest of us assembled there. I recognized him immediately as the farm's General Manager. The same individual who had earlier accepted my application, interviewed me and ultimately, offered me the job. He stepped to the head of the table in the middle of the room.

"Good mornin'," he said with a measure of forced energy and authority. Some of the full time employees responded. Most didn't. Those of us chosen as the summertime crew simply cowered. The General Manager seemed unfazed by the lack of enthusiastic response. I guessed this scene played itself out regularly.

"I hope everybody had a good, restful weekend, because we've got a lot of work to do," he began. Without further pleasantries, he proceeded to highlight the major projects for the week ahead. I listened intently, understanding little. Finally, he got to the agenda item that most interested me.

"Now, I want to take a minute to welcome the group of young men who will be joining us for the summer," he said, motioning in our direction. "I won't take the time to introduce 'em to ya now, but I'm sure we'll all get to know each other well before the summer is over. I have met with my foremen and we are ready to make department assignments for the summer help. As I read off your name, join the appropriate foreman and he'll take ya to where you'll be working." The men who had accompanied him into the room stepped away from the walls against which they had been leaning. Each seemed to make an effort to stand slightly taller now.

One by one the names of my counterparts were called. Each stepping forward at the appropriate time.

"Ronnie Williamson and Jeff Alsobrook. Y'all will be working in grounds maintenance. William Bannister will be your supervisor."

With those simple words, Ronnie and Jeff began a full summer of activities centered around mowing, trimming, painting and other odd jobs.

In less than two minutes, all of the names had been called and the assignments made. Every name, that is, except mine. I now stood uncomfortably alone.

"Let's see. Who've we got left? Oh, yeah, Phillip Van Hooser. Van Hooser, you'll be joining Earl and his crew on the hill."

My eyes met those of my new supervisor. He grinned mischievously, extended his index finger toward me, turned his palm heavenward, and motioned for me to join him.

"Come on boy, we've got work to do," he said good naturedly, as he turned and exited through the break room door. I hurried across the room to catch up. I found him waiting for me just outside the break room door.

Earl was of average build, probably just under six feet tall.

I guessed him to be in his early fifties. The cap he wore, an obvious freebie, sported a sewed on Purina Mills patch and set slightly cocked on the right side of his head. The cowboy boots he wore were noticeably soiled. I should have immediately recognized this tell tale barnyard clue. I didn't. He extended his hand.

"Phil, my name's Earl Porter. You can call me Earl. Everybody else does." We shook hands. "We're glad to have ya with us this summer. I understand you're quite a hand when it comes to workin' livestock. That'll come in handy this summer on the hill. As a matter of fact, we plan to make ya the 'King of the Slab'." He chuckled mischievously.

Immediately, I began to worry. Quite a hand working with livestock? What was he talking about? My experience with livestock had been limited to raising a few litters of pigs and working with a half dozen head of cattle on our little farm.

"I need to straighten this out right now," I thought. But, before I could say anything, Earl began again.

"Phil, come on over here and meet the other guys in the department." I followed closely as Earl walked toward the gravel parking lot where two military issue jeeps, both painted Kentucky Wildcat blue, and another blue flatbed truck sat parked. Standing beside the truck were four men.

"Fellas, I want y'all to meet our help this summer. This is Phil. Phil's worked livestock before." They all looked sufficiently unimpressed. Earl turned his attention back to me.

"Phil, this here is Tommy Dyer." A heavyset man in his thirties, with dark hair and a contagious smile, took my hand and shook vigorously. "Glad to meet ya, Phil," he said.

In like manner, Earl introduced me to the other three individuals. Bear Holloman...a muscular, friendly, high-energy man in his mid twenties. Buddy Dunning...a quiet man in his mid to late forties. Finally, Eurie Oliver...a man in his mid to late fifties, and thus the oldest of the crew. The other crew members good naturedly referred to him as "the old man." I never had the courage. To me he was "Mr. Eurie." Mr. Eurie's most distinctive feature was his speech pattern. He was extremely soft spoken. I would soon learn that Mr. Eurie's contribution to a conversation would often result in little more than a frustrating, undecipherable mumble.

These were the gentlemen with whom I was destined to spend my summer. But, what was "the hill" to which they kept referring?

Once the introductions were complete, I climbed into the cab of the truck with Earl for a tour of the farm and an explanation of my duties. I soon learned that "the hill" was the name assigned to the section of the farm dedicated to the animal science department. Earl's department was totally responsible for the care and upkeep of the Experiment Farm's livestock. This included a couple hundred head of mixed breed cattle, several dozen head of hogs and four quarter horses, kept for the purpose of working the cattle and checking fences around the property.

The more I heard, the better this job sounded. I liked working with animals, even though I had never done so on quite this scale. I especially liked the idea of riding horses and getting paid for it. Not once in his explanation of my duties had Earl mentioned mowing, painting, pulling bushes, hauling rocks, chopping out tobacco or many of the other things I had learned to hate about working on the farm. This was beginning to sound like the absolutely perfect job for me. Then the other shoe dropped.

"Phil, now you'll be involved in all these activities to some extent. But, your primary job will be the slab."

"What's the slab?" I asked innocently.

"The slab is where we house about sixty or more pigs, each one of 'em between twenty and fifty pounds. We have 'em separated in fifteen or twenty pens. We call it 'the slab' because it's a slab of concrete that these pigs live on. They're born in farrowin' houses on concrete floors and they live there until they're big enough to be weaned and moved to the slab. Phil, you might as well know that these pigs are different than normal hogs. They may be six to nine months old before their feet ever touch dirt or grass. When they do, some of 'em can't take it. They're just way too high strung. I've seen 'em get so excited that they just fall over dead, for no reason. They can't stand the stress. That's why we call 'em 'stress hogs'."

"But, what do I do with 'em?" I asked.

Earl looked directly at me and smiled a big toothy grin. "Why, you're gonna be the King of the Slab. You're gonna take care of their every need. Ya feed 'em, ya check up on 'em and ya clean up after 'em."

"What do ya mean 'clean up after 'em'?"

"Phil, three or four times a week, every week, for the rest of the summer, you'll be on the slab with a high pressure hose washing down those concrete block pens. It's one of the hottest, nastiest, not to mention smelliest jobs, on the whole farm. But, it's gotta be done and we believe you're the man to do it." He nodded and smiled broadly.

No need for further discussion. I understood perfectly my position in the work world pecking order. What had earlier seemed like a plum job was now showing its true colors—or smells.

Nevertheless, I tried to rise to the occasion. I quickly decided to adopt an optimistic outlook. There had to be a bright side. "If others can do it, so can I," I said to myself. "After all, how bad can it be?"

The answer to that question was clearly revealed less than an hour later, as I found myself involved in my first slab wash. How bad could it be? Bad. Real bad!

Besides the obvious challenge of battling ninety-plus degree temperatures and eighty-plus percent humidity, all the while dressed in a rubber suit, I found myself standing ankle deep in what can be most delicately described as pig poop soup. This isn't exactly what I had in mind when I went searching for the perfect job. I doubted many sixteen year old girls would be terribly impressed by the glamorous world of slab washing. Paint brushes and hay fields were looking better all the time.

To make matters even worse, I was surrounded in each and every pen by four to six aggravating "stress hogs." Even for a pork fanatic like myself, it was almost enough to make me swear off fried pork chops forever. Based on firsthand experiences, I quickly concluded that the term "stress hogs" applied not to their psychological makeup, but rather to what they did to the emotional state of those assigned to hose out their pens.

Time after time, for the next several weeks, I found myself doing battle not only with the heat, the flies and the stinking solution lapping at my ankles, but also with those pesky pigs as they chewed on my pant legs, boot laces and the water hose itself.

On one memorable occasion, an especially irritating hog would simply not leave the hose alone. He would take the hose in his mouth and then run backward, dislodging the hose from my grip. The pressurized hose would then thrash to and fro around the pen, spraying both water and the liquified fecal matter in every direction. For the pig, this was a wonderful diversion. For me, a bad job was made immediately worse.

During one such wrestling match, I jerked the hose to free it from the mouth of my combatant. As I did, the brass nozzle on the hose struck my wristwatch, dislodging the crystal from its face. I watched as it tumbled into the concoction below. Gingerly, I leaned over to retrieve it from the mess. As I did, one of the little porkers rushed forward and scooped it up in his mouth. In less than a second, I heard a sickening crunching sound. He had eaten the crystal from my watch! It was more than I could stand. Involuntary reflex took over.

Without thinking, I flicked the brass nozzle around, striking the pig squarely on his snout. In less time than it took for me to strike out, I knew I had made a terrible mistake. Once struck, the pig stood for a brief instant squealing wildly and then without any further warning, fell over. Dead!

I was shocked. I had not intended to hurt the pig, no matter how frustrated I might have been. It just happened. And now, there he lay.

I must admit that my first desperate thoughts were not for the dearly departed pig. In all honesty, I was worried most about me. My first real job and now I'm responsible for killing one of their precious stress hogs—with a water hose! I was certain that I would be fired for sure.

Quickly, I fell to my knees beside the pig in the horrible muck. Maybe he wasn't really dead. Maybe he was just unconscious. Maybe I could revive him.

Furiously, I pushed on his stomach. I patted his jowls. I raised his head and blew on his snout. (I could not bring myself to give that pig mouth-to-snout resuscitation, even though the thought did cross my mind!) Nothing I did made any difference at all. The fact was simple. The pig was dead. Meanwhile, the other pigs in the pen continued to squeal joyfully, while yanking at my pant legs and shirtsleeves. They were oblivious to the plight of their fallen pen mate. Apparently, life goes on for a stress hog.

For me, I was certain that life was over. At least my fledgling professional life as I knew it. Undoubtedly, this incident would make it to my "permanent file." It was sure to haunt me for the rest of my career. I was doomed.

After a few minutes of remorseful contemplation, I finally concluded that there was nothing left to do but fess up and take my punishment. Oh, I must admit, I considered trying to hide the pig's carcass and pretending that I knew nothing of its demise. But, I realized that such efforts were not only wrong, they would have proven fruitless. Eventually, I would have been found out. After all, I was the King of the Slab.

Slowly, I climbed out of the pen and began the fifty yard walk down to the feed building. I didn't know who I would find or what I would say, but I knew I had to confess.

As I entered the door of the feed building, I noticed Mr. Eurie emptying the last of a batch of hog feed from the feed bin. I approached him sheepishly. He looked me up and down suspiciously, silently sizing up my unusually rank, disheveled appearance.

"Mr. Eurie, could ya come up to the slab for a minute?" I asked.

"Why?" was his short, barely audible reply.

"Oh, I'd like for ya to take a look."

I simply couldn't bear to tell him that the pig was dead.

He looked at me and mumbled something that I didn't understand. I knew better than to ask him to repeat it. As he brushed past me on his way to the slab, I decided to follow a few feet behind. With each step, I prayed we would find the first resurrected pig in recorded history.

Upon arriving at the pen in question, I motioned for Mr. Eurie to look inside. He approached the gate and leaned forward, eyeing the unquestionably dead pig. Standing silently, without moving, he continued to look at the pig for what seemed to be a very long time. Finally, I felt I had to break the silence. I was afraid that if I didn't, he might start asking the questions that I dreaded most.

"Mr. Eurie, what do ya think we should do?" I asked meekly. His answer was quick, but totally unintelligible. I cringed. I didn't want to ask him the second time, but there was no other way.

"I'm sorry, Mr. Eurie, I couldn't hear ya. What do ya think we should do?"

He whirled around to face me. His answer was unmistakable this time.

"I think YOU should bury the little stressed out S.O.B.!"

With those words and what I think was a little wink, Mr. Eurie walked past me, on his way back to the feed building. Not then, nor at any other time thereafter, did he ask me for more details.

What, without question has been the single dirtiest, nastiest, most unpleasant job I've ever held, has also proven to be one of the best learning experiences. It has had a lasting impact on me. For three straight summers I returned to the Experiment Farm knowing that I would resume my reign as King of the Slab, with all its dubious distinctions. But, why?

First, I came to realize that if I could mentally condition myself to be willing to do the dirtiest, nastiest, most undesirable jobs that anyone could throw at me—the jobs that others thought they were too good to do—then there would always be something available for me to fall back on, if necessary. Life isn't perfect. Life is what we make it. If we sit around waiting for the perfect job, or spouse, or house, or situation to find us, then, more likely than not, we will miss some valuable learning experiences.

Secondly, I came to understand that long-term success is not built on one flawless accomplishment after another. For most of us, long term success is realized through the on-going process of trial and error. We try, we fail. We acknowledge our mistakes, face the consequences and learn from them.

Oh, yeah. Then we pause just long enough to bury our mistakes before we move on.

It took Mr. Eurie to teach me that.

"Life is a long lesson in humility."

JAMES M. BARRIE

7

Battle Scars

I can't remember having to contend with many specific fears as a child. My life was fairly secure. Oh, I had a healthy respect for snakes, poisonous or not. But, as long as I could see them and knew where they were, I didn't really fear them. I didn't especially like the dark, but I was never left alone, outdoors, after dark anyway. I suppose I had an occasional childhood nightmare or two that I had to cope with. But, I soon learned that most of them were temporary and simply the lingering after effects of an especially spine tingling episode of *The Twilight Zone.*

No, I didn't fear very many things at all. However, as I grew out of childhood and entered my high school years, one thing occupied an inordinate amount of my "worry time." Simply stated, I desperately dreaded getting stitches.

When I have summoned the courage to confess this foolish fear to individuals in the past, I have actually found several that could empathize with me. They admitted that they, too, feared stitches. But, almost to a person, each would eventually admit that it wasn't the stitches that really unnerved them, but rather the anticipation of the preliminary injections necessary to deaden the pain.

That was not my situation. Injections—shots—were of no concern to me at all. Beginning at the age of five or six, I took allergy shots, as often as weekly, for years. No, the injections were the least of my concerns. For me, it was the stitches themselves that I reflected on.

My first concern was the vivid mental picture that I had created regarding the process of having flesh mended. I recall one Sunday morning when my three year old brother, Mark, fell from his spring-loaded rocking horse, face first, onto a concrete porch. The tumble caused him to bite through his lower lip. I remember the initial blood, tears and general confusion. What I remember most though, was the story I later heard of how the emergency room doctor suggested to my parents that Mark be wrapped in a sheet and thereby totally immobilized, so the doctor could repair the damage unimpeded.

Daddy wouldn't hear of it. Instead, Daddy clearly explained to Mark what was about to happen. He stressed that Mark would need to lie very still in order for the doctor to do his job. As a result, Mark did just that. The damage was repaired and no sheet, or any other constraint, was necessary. I always marveled at the imagined courage and determination it took for Mark to be so brave and focused in that situation. I worried, I guess, down deep, that should a situation arise calling for such bravery, discipline and self-control on my part, I simply wouldn't be able to conjure up the same tensile strength of internal metal.

The second reason I feared stitches so, was the visible scars—those lasting calling cards representing previous problems and misfortunes. Now, I'm not referring to vanity issues relative to scarred appearances. Most of us would agree that some of the most devastating scars are those not visible to the naked eye. Yet, many can be seen. For visible scars, I had always been concerned with what I referred to as an individual's "pain equation." For every scar there was a story. Each story involved an element of emotional suffering—pain recalled. Therefore, I logically assumed that the possibility existed that every time an individual looked at their scars, the pain of the experience was, in some measure, relived. The result? Over time, the reliving of the painful experiences would multiply their emotional impact.

But, these were not the type of issues that hot-blooded seventeen year old males talked about freely and openly. Fears? Publicly, we weren't afraid of anything.

My high school years had quickly slipped by. Since elementary school, I had looked forward with great anticipation to being a high school jock. For a time during my early teens, I even harbored certain fantasies about becoming a professional athlete. However, by the time I reached my junior and then senior years in high school, I had come to the more realistic conclusion that grand achievements in the arena of sports were not reserved for me. I had to face facts. I was at best an average athlete.

Not that being average is bad. After all, average is where most of us fall. I have realized over the years that "above average" and "exceptional" are adjectives reserved for a select few. As it relates to sports, those who earn above average consideration are those who are usually bigger, faster, stronger and more talented than most. I wasn't any of those. I was again, average. Average size, average speed, average strength, average talent.

If I was above average in any way, it would have been in the area of desire. Here is an interesting fact I have discovered which applies to both the activity of sports and life itself. When surrounded by other average individuals, those average folks who are able to perform with heightened levels of desire and personal drive, as compared to the other average individuals around them, are often judged to be above average, sometimes good and occasionally, even great. The reward? They are provided more opportunities to perform and prove themselves than their equally average, though less driven, counterparts. Under such circumstances, it is not at all unusual for these driven folks to grow and evolve into consistently above average, good and even great performers. The lesson to be learned? Drive yourself. Always.

As I said before, my high school football career was quickly drawing to an end. I loved playing the game. I found almost every aspect of the experience to be enjoyable: the team aspect, the competition, the discipline required, the physical nature of the contests, almost everything. However, as the end drew near, I began to realize that I had never really distinguished myself.

I never made the all-conference squad, much less all region or all state, and now I was sure I never would. Such public recognition was reserved for the exceptional athletes.

Oh, I had fleeting moments of fame and infamy alike. For example, a few isolated plays found me in the right place at the right time. Plays that brought momentary applause, accolades and personal recognition. I clearly remember the bone jarring, open field solo tackle that I made on an attempted punt return in the Trigg County game. I also vividly remember the improvised pass play that quarterback, Steve Kukahiko and I devised in the contest against Hopkinsville High. The result was a pass he threw which I caught and carried eighty-one yards for a touchdown and a new school record. Those were exciting moments.

But, in all honesty, I remember depressing failures even more clearly. For example, I clearly remember the sickening feeling that engulfed me as I watched the Mayfield High running back sweep around my end and scamper into the end zone for a touchdown. His touchdown provided the margin for his team's victory, simply because I had allowed myself to be blocked.

Such was the nature of my football career. A series of plays, some good and some bad, but none of them truly representative of how I wanted to remember my football experience and the way I approached the game.

So, now, here I stood with one last chance to make an impact. To leave a lasting impression. Having played the game since fifth grade, I now faced the last half of the final football game of my career. And I knew it.

Less than ten minutes earlier, during the closing comments of their half time pep talk, the coaches had reminded the underclassmen that this was the end of the season. Whatever happened in the second half of this game would stay with them until play resumed the following year.

For those of us who were seniors, the message was significantly different. There would be no "Wait 'til next year!" rallying cry for us. This was the final opportunity—the end of our careers. What did or didn't happen on the field in the second half, would stay with us for the rest of our lives. The motivation was simple. It was either now or never.

Simple as it was, it was all the motivation I needed. I vowed within myself, to make this last half of football something I could be proud of forever.

With that vow driving my thoughts and soon my actions, I stood anxiously, pawing at the dirt with my cleats, awaiting the second half kickoff. As I dug in at the twenty yard line, I watched our opponents, the Christian County Colonels, begin to position themselves, opposite us, at the other end of the field. I could hardly wait to get started. I was determined to give everything I had in this second half! I wouldn't, I couldn't, hold anything back. This was my final opportunity to prove to myself, my family, my teammates, my school and my community that I was worthy to represent them on this field. It was time to rise to the occasion. This occasion.

In the last few seconds before kickoff, I mentally reviewed my responsibilities one final time.

"When the ball is kicked, follow the flight of the ball to make sure that the deep kickoff return men have fielded the ball cleanly. When they get the ball, lead the ball carrier into the middle of the field, through the wedge that the linemen will be forming. Block any opponent who may penetrate the wedge. If all blocking assignments are carried through properly, it's possible to return this opening kickoff for a touchdown," I thought.

I was ready. I watched intently as the Christian County kicker carefully placed the football on the tee. I watched as the referee quickly conducted a final head count of all the players on the field...nineteen, twenty, twenty-one, twenty-two. All ready. I heard the shrill blast from his whistle as he thrust his arm downward, signaling the beginning of play. I focused on the kicker as he jogged toward the ball positioned on the kicking tee. At precisely the right instant, he planted his left foot in the turf and swung his right leg and foot toward the ball. The foot connected solidly with a dull thud, and the ball rocketed upward in an end over end fashion.

The second half, my final half, was under way.

As instructed, I watched intently the flight of the football as it left the tee and approached the apex of its flight. My teammates began rushing to their predetermined positions around the field, in anticipation of the coming onslaught of Christian County players. Collisions began to occur all over the playing field. Still, anxiously I stood watching the flight of that football.

As I watched the football reach the top of its arch, and begin its tumbling motion earthward, everything suddenly seemed to shift into a slower motion. As I watched the path of the ball carefully, I calculated that it was headed directly toward me. Its destination was unmistakable. I quickly realized that my former responsibilities were no longer appropriate. I could not afford to let the ball drop near me, in hopes that one of the designated kickoff return specialists would retrieve it. I had to field the ball and return this kickoff.

As the ball approached, one final, fleeting thought raced through my mind.

"This is it," I thought. "This is the reason I am here tonight. This is my opportunity to prove myself worthy."

As such thoughts raced through my mind, the football arrived. I watched carefully its final descent, until it hit with a thud between the royal blue four and the three emblazoned on my jersey. Instinctively, both hands closed around the ball. Once secured, I shifted the ball to my right hand and cradled it protectively in the space between my arm and my rib cage.

Quickly, I lowered my center of gravity and began running up field in search of the wedge and my lead blocker. A quick glance to my left and I immediately noticed the blocking wedge taking shape, as planned, in the middle of the field. I veered left toward the wedge, gaining speed and momentum. Still no lead blocker. But, I couldn't wait. By now, all my senses were engaged. I watched as I ran. There was movement on every side. Bodies strewn everywhere as the defense worked desperately to break through the wedge to contain me and the ball.

Then I saw it! It was unexpected and beautiful. In the midst of all the chaos, I saw an opening. About seven yards to my right. An uncontested opening, through which I could clearly see Christian County's end zone about sixty yards away. Without thinking, I cut sharply back right, headed for the opening, abandoning the security of the wedge and its blockers. "All I have to do is get through that opening," I thought, "and then the prize will go to the swiftest." I somehow sensed that Caldwell County High School football immortality lay waiting a mere sixty yards away.

As I reached the opening, suddenly, without warning, I felt immersed in total darkness. All light was blotted out. For the next few seconds, I experienced nothing but eery silence and pain.

I don't remember the tackle itself. My memories of it were formed a few days later, after watching it over and over on film. However, the images accompanying "the hit" are inescapable. There, in the darkness of the viewing room, I would watch the flickering photographic images as, Pat Gates, one of Christian County's premier players, and I viciously collide just after I had made my cut toward the opening. I watched carefully, the projector running in slow motion, as he executed a textbook tackle. With head lowered, he thrust his body forward, driving his head gear directly into my chest, while simultaneously wrapping his arms around my lower back. Once the physically larger Gates' arms were securely wrapped, he would hoist my body upward and then drive it to the ground. As my head and shoulders struck ground first, his helmet slid off my chest and directly into my chin. Finally, gravity ensured that we both tumbled to the ground, as the referee blew his whistle signaling the end of the play.

But, all that information was still a few days down the road. No, I don't remember the tackle, but I vividly remember its crushing power and its immediate aftereffect. As I lay on my back, initially dazed, I began to regain use of the senses, which had been temporarily interrupted. My first thought involved my chest and breastbone, which I was certain had been crushed. With the blow, much of the air from my lungs was gone, having been forcibly deflated. I lay still, eyes closed, gasping for breath. At that moment, unfortunately, my sense of hearing began to return.

"Way to go, Pat!" I heard his teammates yelling enthusiastically.

I was certain then and I'm certain now that there was nothing malicious in regard to the tackle. Football is a physical game. It's designed to be played that way. I'm sure that Gates was proud of the tackle. I certainly would have been had it been the other way around.

But, then I heard the words that served as the specific motivation I needed to get up off the ground.

"Great hit, man! He's hurt. He ain't comin' back."

Gates had done his job, now it was time for me to do mine. Slowly, I rolled over on my side. As I pushed myself up onto my hands and knees, I began to draw deeper breaths. Finally, I was on my feet, staggering back to the huddle.

As the game officials worked to establish the official placement of the football and the chains, I used those precious extra seconds to rejoin my teammates. My initial concern for my chest had passed as the air began returning to my lungs. However, it had been replaced with an ever-growing concern for my chin and jaw. As I had been sure my chest had been crushed a moment before, I was now just as certain that my jaw was broken. But, I didn't dare rub it in clear view of our opposition.

Once again hidden and anonymous within the security of the huddle, I began to take a quick physical inventory. Unbuckling the chinstrap on my helmet, I quickly reached up and began to move my chin backwards and forwards, up and down. Everything seemed to work as it had been originally designed. However, as I withdrew my hand, I noticed a significant amount of blood on my palm. I glanced down and noticed the bold contrast between the red blood spilling from my chin against the white road jersey that I wore. I turned to the teammate on my right and his nonverbal reaction made me know that the cut was significant. I turned to head for the sidelines, but it was too late. Steve Kukahiko was already in the process of calling the next play. So, quickly I buckled my chinstrap and took my position. At the snap of the ball, I simply went through the motions of what I was supposed to do, making sure to avoid contact of any kind. As soon as I heard the whistle blow, signaling the end of the play, I headed directly for the sideline and medical attention.

Before I could make it all the way to the sideline and the team physician, I was intercepted on the field by our head coach, Al Giordano. As he rushed toward me, he latched onto my arm. I heard him ask excitedly, "Van Hooser, where ya think you're goin'?"

By now, I figured it should have been obvious to just about everyone where I was going. Blood stains covered my chinstrap and the front of my jersey. Bloody prints were evident on my pants where I had attempted to wipe the gooey liquid from my hands after applying direct pressure to the cut.

"I'm gonna get the doctor to look at my chin," I shouted anxiously.

"Don't worry about your chin for a couple of minutes. It'll keep," he said, as he shoved his hand into his back pants pocket and retrieved a new roll of white athletic tape, about two inches wide. "I've gotta play I want ya to tell Kukahiko to run." Then as if he sensed my hesitancy, he added, "Son, we need ya in there on this one."

I nodded, indicating my willingness to accept the assignment. Quickly, he tore off a four or five inch strip of the tape and applied it directly to the cut under my chin. As he worked, he explained the play to me. I recognized it immediately. It was the same play we had practiced several times during the previous week. Coach Giordano seemed convinced that this was the perfect moment to execute the play.

With tape securely in place and instructions complete, Giordano released his death grip on my arm. I raced back onto the field. Upon reaching the huddle, I breathlessly relayed the play to Kukahiko. He recognized the play quickly and flashed an encouraging smile, before turning his attention to the huddle.

"Halfback option pass left. Linemen, be sure to hold your blocks and DON'T release and go downfield. No penalties. On two. Ready, break!"

Kukahiko's instructions were crisp and definitive. Each player understood what he was expected to do. Each player understood the potential of this play.

Our halfback that night was freshman, David Barnes. David was young, small and inexperienced. It's doubtful that his name had ever been mentioned in one of Christian County's practices or during any of their film sessions. There would have been no reason for the Colonels' coaching staff to be concerned with him at all. We were betting heavily that they didn't know much about him or his tendencies. We were betting that they didn't know he was left handed. The time had come to unleash the element of surprise.

As we broke from the huddle, I slowly jogged to my receiver's position at the split right end. Out of the corner of my eye, I watched my defender eye me suspiciously. It was obvious that I was hurt. Blood stains covered my uniform. I must have looked a mess. As I positioned myself across the line from him, I stared downward, trying to appear totally unconcerned about the play, while I rubbed my still bleeding chin.

"DOWN! SET!" Kukahiko shouted, our players took their positions. "HUT ONE, HUT TWO!"

On the count of two, the ball was snapped and players on both sides of the line moved quickly. Kukahiko took the ball, whirled around, and pitched it quickly to the halfback, Barnes, who had flared toward the left sideline. He caught the ball cleanly and tucked it against his left side, while continuing to run toward the sidelines. From all indications, it appeared to be a traditional end sweep.

In the meantime, at the snap of the ball, I headed straight downfield in what amounted to no more than a lazy trot. My defender glanced at me quickly. Noting my obvious lack of hustle and the action taking place on the opposite side of the field, he hesitated ever so briefly, then took one step toward the line of scrimmage. It was all I needed. At that precise moment, I accelerated, quickly sprinting past him and angling across the middle of the field toward the left corner of the end zone. He immediately realized that he had been snookered. When Barnes saw my cut, he pulled up, set his feet and lifted the football above his left shoulder.

"PASS! PASS!" defenders all over the field were shouting frantically.

But, it was too late. Barnes lifted a high arching pass that fluttered downfield toward me. This time I was not thinking of personal glory, injuries or anything else. This time my singular focus was on catching the ball.

As the ball started its downward flight, I could tell that it was slightly over thrown. I didn't know if I could catch up to it or not. Finally, at the last possible instant, I thrust my right hand forward as far as I possibly could without overextending myself and tumbling face first into the grass. As the nose of the football struck the tips of my fingers of my outstretched hand, for one precious nanosecond of time, it stuck to my blood covered fingers. It stuck just long enough to allow me to reach forward with my left hand and secure possession of the ball. Once the ball was securely in my grasp, I ran the last several yards untouched, into the end zone for a touchdown.

By the time the official's arms were raised signaling a touchdown, momentary pandemonium had broken out in the end zone. Hugs. Smiles. Cheers. High fives all around. The celebration was spontaneous and sincere. It was glorious.

After the game, I sat in a more subdued locker room. The

game was now complete and the earlier cheers were already just a memory. My thoughts began to drift to my next activity for this evening. Soon, I would be leaving for the Caldwell County War Memorial Hospital to have the still gaping cut in my chin stitched up. But, somehow it wasn't my chin, or the coming stitches that occupied my mind. Instead, my mind revolved around the bittersweet feelings that I was experiencing related to a part of my life just ending. As I sat, absorbed in my thoughts, Coach Giordano approached the bench on which I sat.

"Van Hooser, ya played a good game tonight," he said quietly.

"Thanks," I mumbled.

"How's the chin?"

"Awright, I guess."

Then Coach G said something I have not forgotten and I doubt that I ever will.

"Son, for the rest of your life, every morning when ya shave, you'll remember this night. That scar will be a constant reminder of a commitment ya made. It'll remind ya that ya were willin' to pay the price."

I can't honestly say that I have thought of that night *every* time I have shaved since then. But, I can say that I have thought about it hundreds of times. I've thought about it because of what it taught me. I now understand that when we play, participate or commit to anything worthwhile, there is a price to be paid. Sometimes the price is high. Sometimes the price requires pain. Sometimes it leaves scars.

I am no longer fearful of stitches, or the scars that leave a lasting reminder of their existence. As strange as it may seem, now I'm fearful that I won't get any more. I fully realize that some people strive to avoid any possibility of pain and discomfort that competition and life may bring, by quitting, by bailing out, before the battles begin. Certainly, that is an option. But, what I've learned is that by digging in, hanging on and working *through* such situations, personal victories can be won. I now realize that scars can serve as a testament to our individual commitment and personal resilience. In a very real sense, our battle scars from life become our personal medals of honor.

"The only real losers in life are people who end their lives having tasted neither victory nor defeat."

THEODORE ROOSEVELT

8

Uncle Harvey

Everyone has an Uncle Harvey.

Or at least they would like to.

Since becoming an uncle myself more than twenty-five years ago, I have been on a quest to discover the recipe for successful "unclehood." What is it that makes some uncles memorable, even lovable, while others remain simply tolerable? In my mind, I am convinced that distinctive qualities, or at the very least, specific characteristics distinguish the revered uncle (or aunt) from the average, run-of-the-mill variety.

If my contention is sound, then I would like to offer several possible characteristics for consideration. My first offering would be the issue of intellect.

Certainly, no one wants an uncle who is dumb as a coal bucket. Clear, original thoughts and the ability to communicate independent, unique ideas are appealing. Yet, there is a delicate balance that must be maintained. Too much effort expended to prove superior intellect may serve to drive potentially adoring nieces and nephews away in droves. Most of us have, at some point, experienced firsthand the dreaded encounters with "know-it-all" relatives. The memories can prove to be gruesome.

For me, another fascinating personal characteristic for uncles has always been the magnetic appeal associated with the breadth of one's varied life experiences. Even as a young child, I could sit for hours on end in rapt fascination listening to individuals share personal adventures which recounted episodes ranging from the risky to the ridiculous. I loved to live vicariously through the storyteller.

For example, I marveled at the personal self confidence that must have been required for my father, then a mere sixteen years old, to leave the cocoon-like security of Farmersville, Kentucky, to ride a train almost three thousand miles across the United States, mysteriously drawn by the previously unknown sophistication of San Francisco, California. He set out, with his own father's words of admonition ringing in his ears, "Boy, if ya get sick or hurt let us know. But, if ya get out there and run out of money or get yourself in trouble, don't call me 'cause I ain't coming out there to bail ya out."

On other occasions, I would sit mesmerized listening to my Uncle Frog's wartime experiences as a belly gunner during World War II.

I was enchanted by the scope of domestic travel my Uncle Roy unknowingly punctuated for me when he would display his United States atlas. Why? Because, over the years, he had painstakingly highlighted literally every road he had traveled from the Pacific to the Atlantic and from Canada to Mexico.

I laughed loud and long when my eighty-something year old Uncle Dood finally relented after years of silence on the matter and shared his youthful experience of voluntarily riding with a friend in a horse drawn wagon from his Farmersville home to Bowling Green, Kentucky. A journey of almost ninety miles, made considerably more unpleasant because it was undertaken in the midst of a snowstorm. When pressed as to why he would tackle such a foolish adventure, my uncle the unwavering teetotaler, meekly admitted that alcohol had been involved.

The ability and willingness of these loved ones to share personal experiences with those of us representing the next generation, regardless of how dangerous, adventurous, or embarrassing these experiences might be, without question enhanced my feelings for them. It proved that they were human. Their stories demonstrated their zest for life in ways that the rest of us might otherwise never have known.

Yes, life experiences are certainly a plus, but all our lives are an accumulation of experiences. There must be more that will elevate one to favored status.

Maybe it was human flaws. It has always been easier for me to relate to human imperfection, than feigned perfection. From a personal standpoint, I have had more experience with imperfection. Individuals who have failed, but haven't faltered or foundered, encourage me. Their resilience, their sense of the need to "keep on keepin' on" is personally attractive. They seem to be able to use temporary failures as stepping stones, not stumbling blocks, which lead from one adventure to the next.

But, if I were ranking the characteristics that I find most appealing, without hesitation, number one on my list would be a healthy sense of humor. The ability to laugh at things truly laughable <u>and</u> the ability to find humor when an otherwise humorless void exists.

Each of these characteristics is attractive in its own right. But, on those rare occasions when all three—intelligence, personal experiences and a healthy sense of humor—converge in one human being, the result is remarkable. Without question, it's memorable. For me, that unique individual was my Uncle Harvey.

The man, Harvey Loughrie, was very average when measured by conventional standards. Physically, he was not especially outstanding. He would have easily settled into a crowded mall or auditorium with very little attention being paid to him. When passing him on a sidewalk, I doubt that many people paused to steal a second look.

Already in his mid forties at the time of my birth, I distinctly recall a bespectacled man with a graying mustache. He was of average height and weight. His most obvious distinguishing feature, without question, would have been his hair. Or more accurately, the lack of it. The top of his head was slick. What little hair that did exist on the sides and back of Uncle Harvey's head, he kept clipped short and was therefore of little consequence.

He was also one of the first true Yankees that I had ever known. A native of Ohio, he didn't speak, or think for that matter, like the rest of us. I suppose he was the first member of our extended family to have attended college, Kent State University. This remarkable distinction was realistically reserved for a small percentage of men his age during the late 1940's. In simple terms, Uncle Harvey was a bit different and he never tried to hide the fact.

His experiences were of a different variety as well. I am convinced that for every fascinating detail that I might be able to recall and relate concerning Uncle Harvey, dozens of others exist still undiscovered by me. But, a few of the more prominent ones come to mind.

Uncle Harvey was a proud Army veteran. He was unlucky enough to be born during a period of global unrest, but fortunate enough to be born with an uncommon reservoir of courage and resilience that allowed him to step forward and serve his country proudly and with considerable distinction. A desperate period of Uncle Harvey's military experience was spent in the Italian theater during the height of World War II. During this campaign, Uncle Harvey was wounded in some untold battle on some long-forgotten mountain in Italy. During the battle sequence, an explosion occurred close to Uncle Harvey. He was temporarily blinded. Having escaped more serious injury, Uncle Harvey was luckier than many of his comrades that day. All around him were serious, life threatening, debilitating injuries which required a level of medical care not available at the battle's front. However, evacuation of these wounded, during battle conditions, proved even more challenging.

Due to the hazardous mountain terrain in which they were located and the hostile environment surrounding them, the wounded and incapacitated had to be removed from that mountain on the backs of sturdy, sure footed donkeys. These beasts of burden were capable of traversing long, steep, narrow mountain trails. As the wounded were loaded one by one, onto the backs of these animals, Uncle Harvey found himself in yet another tenuous position. As fellow soldiers and wounded friends were seated or positioned aloft, there was no beast available for Uncle Harvey. He would have to stay.

Finally, a compassionate and enterprising medic provided an adventurous alternative for my uncle.

"Loughrie, we hate to leave you up here, but there's no room for you on the donkeys. The rest of these guys can't walk. If you want to come along, you're going to have to grab the tail of one of those donkeys and just hold on. Be sure to stay close to the side of the mountain, because if you drift too far from behind your donkey, you might just step off the side of the mountain. Then, you're a goner for sure."

With no other more attractive options available to him, Uncle Harvey chose to "grab this opportunity by the tail and hang on 'til the end." He literally stumbled blindly, step by step down that mountainside to safety. As he would share the story many years later, I could almost feel the sharp, jagged rocks of the mountain side trail as Uncle Harvey recounted how they dug into his face, neck and shoulder as he over compensated, fearing the possibility that one misplaced step would cause him to plunge over the cliff's edge. Even as a youngster, I could sense the desperation that must have enveloped him.

Not that Uncle Harvey would let on. Before I or any other listener was allowed to slip into an uncomfortable state of despair associated with his plight, Uncle Harvey would allow his sense of humor to surface. With a mischievous look in his eye, he would finish by saying, "As a result of that one experience, I've learned that the best way to get through difficult periods in life is to find the biggest ass available and follow closely."

Without exception, regardless of the story, situation or circumstance, with Uncle Harvey, laughter was the end result. It was always that way. We laughed not so much at Uncle Harvey's words, but rather we laughed in awe of his ability to find the humor in a situation so dire that even survival itself was occasionally in question. That was the special quality, the uniqueness of Uncle Harvey. It seemed to be his attitude toward life: *Take whatever life deals you. Don't whine and bellyache. Use humor as your ally and deal with it!*

Uncle Harvey had many opportunities to apply this attitude. In many ways, he lived a very challenging life. More so than most.

He experienced loss. While still a young man in his twenties, Uncle Harvey's first wife was killed in an automobile accident, while on her way to pick him up from work. He was left with the daunting challenge of recovering from the emotional loss, while still raising their young son that was left behind. True to form, he rebounded nicely, marrying my Aunt Ruth (my father's sister) and fathering five more children, three girls and two boys.

He experienced isolation. Following his World War II military service, in the mid fifties, Uncle Harvey, now working in a Civil Service position, accepted an assignment at a remote weather station located at the North Pole. His specific duties remain unclear to me to this day. But, what is clear is that for twenty-four out of the next twenty-five months Uncle Harvey endured dreadful isolation and separation from family, friends and civilization. Yet, his wit and imaginative spirit never forsook him.

He experienced pain. Some of the most serious challenges faced by Uncle Harvey were physical in nature. During his period of military service, there was the blindness episode. In middle age, he lost a majority of his stomach to a surgical procedure. As time passed, circulation problems became his primary burden, culminating in the required amputation of one leg. Yet, he faced each of these physical trials with his unique sense of humor intact.

I remember the first time I saw Uncle Harvey after his amputation. I was working and living out of the area and did not see him until after he had been fitted with his plastic prosthesis—his new leg.

I was visiting my parents when Uncle Harvey, Aunt Ruth and their oldest son, David, stopped by. It was rather awkward and uncomfortable for all of us at first. It had only been a few short weeks since his leg had been removed and we imagined that he was still dealing with the physical and emotional trauma of the ordeal.

As he entered the house, I noticed the considerable difficulty he was having in balancing and walking on his new leg. Even though he showed no outward signs of suffering, I was concerned that physical pain was still a primary factor. For some reason, I temporarily discounted the medicinal value of Uncle Harvey's wit and humor.

As Uncle Harvey settled into the recliner next to the couch, I attempted small talk.

"Uncle Harvey, how ya doin'?" I began.

"Oh, about as good as can be expected for anybody surrounded by this many Van Hoosers."

We laughed. Same old Uncle Harvey. Feeling a little more at ease, I decided to be more specific.

"How's the leg doin'?"

"I don't know, I haven't seen it in a while," was his immediate, sarcastic response. "But I think this new one they gave me will work out fine just as soon as I learn to balance on it. I should be dancing again any day now," he said with a smile.

"Is there any pain?"

"Well, it hasn't been too bad." I was sure that this was a tremendous understatement, if not an outright lie. He continued. "But I must say, for some reason my 'good foot' is hurting me this morning."

It was very unlike Uncle Harvey to offer such an obvious complaint. Immediately, almost involuntarily, all of us in the room cast our eyes toward Uncle Harvey's feet. In a matter of seconds, my youngest brother, Dan, about ten years old at the time, blurted out what the rest of us knew to be the unvarnished truth, but for which we were having difficulty finding the right words.

"Well, of course it hurts." Dan observed loudly. "It ought to. Ya got your shoes on the wrong feet!"

An immediate, momentary hush fell over the room. Uncle Harvey leaned forward to survey, firsthand, the situation beneath him. As he glanced at his feet, he started to giggle. Quickly, the rest of us joined him with nervous, supportive laughter.

"Thanks Dan. I don't know why the rest of these Van Hoosers couldn't be as sharp as you."

Dan beamed proudly at the thought of his discovery.

Uncle Harvey then turned his attention to my cousin David.

"Dave, will you help me switch these?"

With no hesitation, David, the dutiful son, was quickly down on his knees in front of his dad. As David began the task of removing both of Uncle Harvey's shoes, the conversation around the room resumed, even though we all were interested in watching David work. We tried not to be too obvious.

Once David had removed the ill-fitting shoes from both feet, he placed the appropriate shoe on Uncle Harvey's "good foot." He measured the laces and then pulled them snugly before tying. He looked up at Uncle Harvey and asked quietly, "How's that, Dad?"

Uncle Harvey looked down at this thoughtful, obedient son, smiled and said softly, "It's fine Dave. Thanks."

With that, David finished tying the shoe and turned his attention to replacing the appropriate shoe on the foot of the prosthesis.

In an attempt to help David in his efforts, Uncle Harvey placed his hands under the prosthesis and raised his new limb slightly as David struggled to slip the shoe on over the sock that was already in place. When the shoe had finally been positioned and fitted correctly, David began the process of tying it.

As he gently measured and then tugged on the laces, Uncle Harvey suddenly let out an unexpected, ear-piercing scream that startled all of us.

David, nearest to his dad, jumped back as if a bomb had gone off under him. Immediately, his eyes went to those of his father.

"Daddy, what's wrong?" David asked breathlessly.

With a twinkle in his eye and sarcasm on his tongue, Uncle Harvey laughed heartily and said, "Can't you tell the laces are too tight. We don't want to cut off the circulation."

It was at that moment that I became convinced that there were few others like my Uncle Harvey...and I want to be just like him.

———

"A man's greatness is not measured by wealth, power or accomplishment. A man's greatness is measured by what it takes to discourage him."

ANONYMOUS

Steppin' Out

*"Do not follow where the path
may lead. Go instead where there
is no path and leave a trail."*

ANONYMOUS

- **J. R.**

- **Christmas in Paris**

- **I'm Gonna Run**

- **Miss Sophie**

9

J. R.

As I burst into the house, Mom and Dad looked up curiously. Mom stared up over the newspaper spread in front of her on the bar. Daddy, coffee cup nearby, momentarily suspended the process of tying his work boots. He raised up to better survey the situation.

"Phil, what's the matter? Are ya awright?" Mom asked, with genuine concern in her voice.

"Oh, I'm fine," I answered sarcastically. "Never better."

I plopped down in one of the chairs at the kitchen table.

We all sat silently for a few seconds.

"Boy, if you're awright, whatta ya doin' home then?" my dad asked more directly.

We all knew I shouldn't be home at this time of the day. Not at 7:25 a.m. Not on a weekday. I should be at work. As a matter of fact, less than forty-five minutes earlier, they had seen me leave for work. Now, for no apparent reason, I was seated in their midst again. Something was wrong. An explanation was warranted. It was my responsibility to provide one. But, I dreaded sharing the details.

"Boy, what's goin' on?" Daddy persisted, his voice dropping an octave or two lower. As he spoke, I could feel his steely blue eyes staring straight at me.

There was no escaping the truth; I might as well get it all out.

"I just quit my job," I blurted out with disgust.

Mom gasped slightly. "Phil, what happened?"

I looked directly at her as I answered, still working to avoid Daddy's eyes.

"I got sick and tired of workin' for that jerk. He jumped on me this mornin' as soon as I got there. I finally got fed up with all his crap and I told him so."

"Phillip Van Hooser, did you get fired?" Mom asked suspiciously.

"No, I didn't get fired. I just told ya, I quit. He prob'ly woulda fired me, but I didn't give him a chance."

"Oh, my..." she said, as her voice trailed off.

We all knew what this meant. I was about four weeks into the summer break from my studies at Murray State University. This summer job was not a luxury for me; it was a necessity. While some of my classmates used their summer to relax, or travel, or even take more classes, none of those were options for me. I needed the money that I would make during the summer to go back to school in the fall. And, this had been a great paying job, too.

For the previous three summers, I had worked at the University of Kentucky's Agricultural Experiment Station in Princeton. They were great people to work for, and they seemed to appreciate my attitude and effort. Earlier in the year, they had offered me the opportunity to return for a fourth consecutive summer. But, I had politely rejected their offer. You see, I got greedy. Several of my buddies had taken various construction jobs in the area that were paying considerably more than I was making at the Experiment Farm. It was obvious that they were doing very well. The dollar signs temporarily clouded my vision. I decided to actively pursue one of those construction-related jobs. That's when I heard about the swimming pool project.

By the summer of 1976, the local Caldwell County political leaders and decision makers had finally decided there was a need for a public swimming pool in Princeton. Funds had been allocated, contractors selected and the basic dirt work begun by the time Murray State's spring semester ended in early May. Upon my return to Princeton, I hurried out to the City/County Park job site to see if positions were available. I was thrilled to learn there were immediate openings for laborers. I was even more excited when I discovered that the starting pay was a whopping $8.19 per hour! More than twice what I had made at the Experiment Station! I didn't need the information I had learned in my recently completed *Algebra and Trigonometry I* class to calculate the financial possibilities. I quickly applied for the job and was hired.

Like most construction jobs, the work was hot, physical and somewhat tedious. For approximately four weeks, I spent my days as a laborer carrying and tying steel rebar reinforcement. Once the reinforced walls and flooring for the pool were sufficiently complete, my responsibilities shifted to concrete work—shoveling, carrying, raking and smoothing wet concrete. It was backbreaking work, all conducted in the bottom of a twelve foot hole.

Physically taxing? Sure. But, that was of little concern to me then. I was in great shape and I enjoyed the activity. The part that I didn't enjoy was my supervisor. He was an out of town contractor who had been brought in to oversee the job. He was the typical autocratic manager—arrogant, abrasive, impulsive, hot headed and totally self-absorbed. I disliked him almost immediately. Yet, I kept reminding myself that it was only for the summer. And the money? I couldn't forget the money. So, for weeks, I had kept my head down and my mouth shut. I worked hard and did my job. All the while, I suffered silently, the barbs and tirades this egomaniac leveled toward my co-workers and me. Then I cut my finger.

During a weekend baseball game, I had torn the little finger on my right hand partially away from the rest of the hand. It was not as gruesome as it may sound, but the injury required several stitches and resulted in considerable swelling in my right hand. My doctor advised me not to do anything with the hand for a week to ten days. Instead, I called the boss, explained my situation and asked if I could have Monday and Tuesday off to let the swelling subside. I assured him I would be back and ready to work on Wednesday. He agreed and said that he understood.

When I arrived for work as planned on Wednesday morning, his mood had changed considerably. There was nothing understanding about him. As I approached the work trailer, the barrage began. He accused me of taking advantage of him and the job. He belittled and berated me. Finally, as this unprovoked tirade continued, he resorted to profanity and name-calling. It was more than I was willing to take. I had never experienced such a situation before. However, I knew I had been taught not to treat others that way and I didn't intend to stand there and take it from him. I stood up to him and then quit. I loaded up my few tools, collected my final check and a few short minutes later I was sitting at Mom and Dad's table, unemployed with approximately eight weeks of summer remaining and no immediate job prospects. My righteous indignation had subsided greatly. Reality and dejection were beginning to set in.

I didn't know exactly what to expect by way of a reaction from my parents. I wasn't concerned about what they would say or do. After all, in my mind, I knew I had done the right thing. Somehow, I believed they would understand. Not just the type of "oh, it will be alright" understanding that parents so often are called upon to offer their children. No, I believed they would understand from a much more practical vantage point. Both my parents had spent the lion's share of their work lives working for someone else. Somehow, down deep, I was confident that they too, had encountered a boss of the sort with which I was having this first experience. If I was right, then they would truly understand that I did what I had to do.

"What are ya gonna do now?" Mom asked.

"I really don't know," I replied honestly and somewhat hopelessly. "I've gotta find somethin' pretty quick. But, I don't even know where to start."

"What about the Experiment Farm?" Mom asked.

"Not a chance. They would have filled their summer openings months ago." I knew their operating procedure too well.

Throughout this brief exchange, Daddy sat quietly.

Thinking. I was anxious to hear his thoughts, to get his input. I needed help.

"Daddy, whatta ya think?" I asked humbly.

"Well, I can't say that I blame ya for doin' what ya did this mornin'," he said simply. "But, I don't know whatta tell ya about a job for the summer. The only thing I can think of is, ya might wanna call J.R. and see if he can use some help."

"J.R." was J.R. Baker, a lifelong friend of Daddy's. I knew J.R., but not well. He owned a farm located in the Creswell community, about three miles "through the bottoms" from Farmersville. On his farm, he raised a field full of goats and not much else. I think he rented out the rest of his farm to others who put out the crops. No, J.R. was no farmer. He was what folks in our area would call a "jackleg carpenter."

The term "jackleg" was not intended to be a derisive one. There were many "jackleg carpenters," "jackleg plumbers," "jackleg mechanics" and so on, scattered throughout our area. This simply meant that the folks practicing these trades were proficient at what they did, however, they usually chose to practice their trade on a relatively small scale and independently. Many were parttime farmers, who enjoyed having the flexibility to work on smaller, less time consuming projects, when they could.

For J.R. it meant that he was usually unwilling to tackle major "finish" carpentry projects, such as new home construction, room additions, or large remodeling projects. Those he left to someone else. Instead, J.R. chose to focus on smaller, usually one-man carpentry projects. Jobs like building a barn, roofing a house, repairing a porch and so on. Just a few years earlier, Daddy had hired J.R. to build a shed on our tobacco barn. I had helped him during that project.

"Do ya think he could use some help?" I asked anxiously.

"I don't know if he could or not. I haven't run in to him in a while so I don't know what he's got goin' on. But, it wouldn't hurt to call him and check."

I knew better than to ask the next question. But, I asked it anyway.

"Daddy, will ya call him for me?" I asked meekly.

"Nope," he said flatly. "I'm not lookin' for a job—you are. If ya wanna know if he needs help, call him yourself." Then with just a little more compassion, he added, "If ya try him right now, ya might still catch him. He usually feeds the goats first thing in the mornin'."

Daddy returned to the process of tying his boots.

The implication was clear. I had asked for help and Daddy had offered a suggestion. Mom had not voiced any reservations. So, the rest was up to me. They had absolutely no intentions of doing it for me. I reached for the phone book and a moment later, was nervously dialing the number.

"Hello?"

"Hello, J.R.?"

"Yeah, this is J.R. Who is this?"

"This is Phillip Van Hooser."

"Who?"

"Phillip Van Hooser. Joe's boy."

"Phillip. Yeah, you're the oldest boy, ain't ya?"

"Yes sir."

"Phil, what can I do for ya this mornin'? Ya wanna buy a goat?"

I chuckled out loud at the thought. I immediately felt better.

"Naw, J.R., I don't need a goat. What I need is a job. I was wonderin' if ya might need any help for the rest of the summer."

"Boy, are ya a carpenter?"

"Not hardly. But, I'll be happy to do whatever I can to help ya out. Maybe I can learn something."

"Son, I can't promise ya a job for the whole summer, but I could use some help roofin' Miss Vera DeBoe's house. You know her, don't ya?"

"Yes, sir. We raised a crop of tobacco on her farm two or three years ago."

"Well, now, lemme tell ya somethin' else. I can only afford to pay ya four dollars an hour. That's all I'm chargin' her. How does that suit ya?"

"It suits me fine," I said, initially trying to mask the disappointment in my voice at the thought of having my pay cut more than fifty percent in less than an hour. Then I remembered that I was without a job. With this job offer, I just got a four-dollar-an-hour raise!

"Boy, when can ya start?"

"Any time."

"Good, I'll see ya there in about an hour. Ya got a hammer?"

"No, sir."

"That's awright, I gotta extra one. See ya in a little while."

With that conversation, I exited the ranks of the unemployed. Momma smiled. Daddy just nodded.

For the next few days, I worked with J.R. on Miss Vera's roofing job, as well as a few other odd jobs that J.R. had already lined up. I was glad to have a job and he seemed happy to have company. We worked steady, but I can't say that we worked terribly hard. J.R. believed in pacing himself. He believed that if you got hot, you owed it to yourself to cool off. He was patient with me and we got along well. The more I was around him and got to know him, the more I grew to like him.

On one occasion, J.R. offered a piece of advice that I remember to this day. We were roofing a house when, out of the blue, J.R. asked me a question.

"Phil, do ya ever think you'll get married?"

The question caught me by surprise. But, by the way he asked the question, I was sure he had a reason for inquiring.

"Yeah, J.R., I expect that I'll take the plunge some day. But, I'm not in any big hurry. Why?"

"Well, I was just workin' on this house and thinkin' that one of these days you'll meet some pretty l'il thing and fall head over heels in love. The next thing ya know, you'll be workin' like a dog to keep her happy and to feed that house full of young'uns that'll be runnin' around. About that time she'll sidle up next to ya one day, real sweet and tell ya that y'all need to build a bigger house. Then off you'll go tryin' to find just the right carpenter to build it for ya. But there will be so many of 'em, you won't know how to pick one from another. That's where I'm about to help ya out, right now. I want ya to line all of 'em up in a row and have 'em hold their hands out. Then I want ya to start countin' their fingers. The ones that have still got all ten—get rid of them. They ain't worth killin'. It's them that's lost a finger or two that'll do ya a good job."

With that, he started laughing as he held out his hands exposing eight fingers, but only one and a half thumbs. I haven't met a carpenter since that day that I haven't done a quick finger count while thinking of J.R.

After working with J.R. for two or three weeks, he came to work one morning with a new proposition for me. He told me that a new church building was being built just over the hill from his house. J.R. explained that one of the church's trustees, a building contractor by the name of Toab Beckner, had called him the night before to see if he wanted to work on the project with them. Because it was so close to J.R.'s house, J.R. had accepted the offer. He went on to assure me that Toab knew about me too, and that Toab was willing to hire me as a carpenter's helper for the balance of the summer at five dollars an hour if I wanted the job. Of course, I was thrilled.

The following Monday morning we were at the church building site, ready to go. The work crew consisted of Toab Beckner, J.R. Baker, Doug Morgan, Billy Graham McCaslin, Joe Van Hooser (not my father, but a distant cousin) and me. All of these men were considerably more experienced as carpenters than me, so the project proved to be an excellent learning experience. The job itself was challenging and enjoyable.

The first week on the job went quickly. Four o'clock, Friday afternoon found us all gathered around Toab's truck, which was parked in what would one day soon be the church parking lot. An informal recap of the week's accomplishments indicated that everybody, especially Toab, was pleased with the progress that had been made. Toab took the time to thank each of us for our efforts on behalf of the church membership.

Then he got around to what I had been looking forward to most. He reached into the glove compartment of the truck and retrieved his checkbook.

"Fellers," he began, "I guess it's about time to settle up for the week."

As he opened the checkbook and prepared his pen, he started, one by one, around the truck, asking each of us how much we were owed. I had no doubt, none whatsoever, that he knew to the penny exactly how much each of us had coming. However, this method was his way of making sure that everyone was treated fairly and that we knew it.

When he had worked his way around the truck hood to me, he asked simply, "Boy, how much do I owe ya?"

"Well, Toab, I worked forty hours at five dollars an hour," I said stating the obvious. "I guess that's about two hundred dollars."

"Fair enough," he said, as he wrote my check.

As he tore my check out of the checkbook, he handed it to me and thanked me once again. Then he turned his attention to J.R.

"J.R., how much do I owe ya?"

"Toab, ya don't owe me nothin'," was J.R.'s shocking reply.

Toab looked directly into J.R.'s eyes for two or three seconds. The men stood facing one another from a distance of less than five feet.

"J.R., are ya sure?" Toab questioned one more time.

"Yeah, I'm sure," was J.R.'s simple reply.

"Well then, thank ya kindly," Toab said, as he turned his attention to the next in line.

A few minutes later, J.R. and I climbed into his truck for the short ride to his house, where my car was parked. I was perplexed. I knew that J.R. was not much of a churchgoer. Yet, I had just watched as he refused payment for a full week's work on a church building. Was there some connection here that I had missed? I knew it was really none of my business, but I felt like I had to ask.

"J.R., I hope ya don't think I'm bein' too nosy; I know it's none of my business. But I was just wonderin' about whatcha told Toab back there. I didn't think ya went to church. But I know ya worked just as hard this week as any of the rest of us. Then ya turn right around and give what amounted to a whole week's salary back to 'em. What's the deal?"

J.R. looked at me and smiled a kind of humble, understated smile.

"Phil, you're right," he said. "I don't go to church much. But, I'd sure hate to live in a community that didn't have one."

His words were simple, straightforward and ever so powerful. He had come to grips with truths that I had not yet realized—there are things that are more important than making money. Often the best time to give is when no one expects you to. And sometimes a person can build something that will last, without the benefit of a hammer.

"Character is what you are when nobody is looking."
ANONYMOUS

10

Christmas In Paris

I awoke early that Christmas morning. The sun had already made its appearance. As I sat up, I noticed my brother, Mark, still sleeping soundly in his bed. I climbed out from under the warmth of my covers and walked quickly to the window of our upstairs bedroom. Still slightly bleary-eyed, I glanced through the window, northward, up Cadiz Street, past the railroad tracks. What I saw encouraged me. The sky was bright and clear. Not a cloud in sight. While I'm certain others around town woke up wishing for a sentimental white Christmas, I was much more practical. Clear, dry weather fit my plans for this day perfectly.

Quickly, I pulled on a pair of well-worn sweat pants and a T-shirt that lay rumpled in the corner. Barefooted, I headed downstairs. As I reached the landing toward the bottom of the stairway, I paused for a moment, glancing across the living room floor at the Christmas tree in the opposite corner. The space beneath the colorfully decorated tree was, as expected, fairly barren. The brightly wrapped packages and gifts that had surrounded, even engulfed this tree less than twelve hours earlier, were now a memory. Their contents already having found their way to closets, tool boxes, cabinets and hope chests all around Caldwell County.

I descended the final two steps into the living room. The house was dark and still. I made my way quietly to the front door. As silently as possible, I unlocked the door and pulled it slowly toward me. As I did, Christmas chimes, the holiday equivalent of wind chimes, began sounding their festive alarm. I had forgotten that Mom had so adorned the door. Startled, I quickly grabbed the clappers and held them firmly in my hand.

Once they were totally muted, I opened the door, this time even more deliberately than before. With the door sufficiently open, I stepped through the opening onto the porch.

As my bare feet left the warmth of the living room carpet and made first contact with the cold, bare concrete porch, I began hopping from one foot to the other, in what could be loosely described as a highly improvised version of an Irish jig. The prancing around caused me to increase my oxygen intake. As I exhaled, I watched the steam from my mouth and nose hang suspended, in the stillness of the morning air, before eventually dissipating into nothingness.

From the porch, I looked straight ahead into a beautiful Kentucky sunrise. The early morning rays caused the ice crystals that had formed overnight on the grass, the trees and the mailbox, to glisten brilliantly. The morning's heavy layer of frost gave evidence that the night had been cold, clear and windless. Perfect!

As my eyes absorbed the beauty around me, I spotted the primary object of my search. The very reason I was dancing on this porch in the first place. The morning's tightly rolled and wrapped issue of *The Louisville Courier Journal* newspaper lay partially hidden in the ditch beyond the sidewalk. I scampered off the porch to retrieve it. With paper in hand, I ran back up the porch steps and immediately removed the paper from its plastic sleeve. Quickly, I began thumbing through the pages until I found what I was looking for. The page containing the area weather map. As I read, it told me exactly what I wanted to hear.

Forecast for Western Kentucky,
West Tennessee and surrounding areas...
Clear today, tonight and tomorrow.
Less than 5% chance of precipitation.
Highs in the low 30's.
Lows in the mid to upper teens.

Quickly, I folded the paper and hurried inside. As I opened

the door, the Christmas chimes loudly and triumphantly signaled my reentry. This time I made no attempt to silence them. As I closed the door behind me, I rubbed my feet furiously on the living room carpet, hoping for some warm relief. As I shuffled there, I was startled by the voice behind me.

"Boy, whatta ya doin' out there?"

I turned quickly around to face the familiar voice. There, at the end of the kitchen table sat my dad in his familiar work pants and undershirt. He didn't have his teeth in and his thinning hair was standing up all over his head.

"Daddy, I didn't hear ya get up," I said, still trying to shake off the chill.

"I just now got up. Whatta ya doin' outside?" he asked again softly.

"I went out to get the paper. Merry Christmas," I said cheerily, as I laid the paper on the table beside him.

"Yeah, thanks," he said with a half chuckle.

"Daddy, ya wanna cup of coffee?" I knew the answer without having to ask the question.

He nodded.

I made my way to the stove and found the well-worn saucepan that I was looking for. It sat in its familiar place on the stove's back left burner. I checked the pan and emptied what little water remained in it from the previous evening. I had often wondered how many hundreds of gallons of water this particular pan had boiled over the years, for coffee one, two, three, or four cups at a time. My mom and dad, and most of their friends, were instant coffee drinkers. Maxwell House Instant Coffee was their brand of choice. They seemed to prefer the convenience and consistency of instant, to its brewed counterparts.

As I half filled the pan with water and sat it on the back burner to heat, I retrieved a cup from the cabinet and a spoon from the drawer. One and a half teaspoons of coffee. Two, three or four teaspoons of sugar. If an error was to be made concerning the sugar, I had learned to err in favor of too much,

rather than too little. That's how he liked it. I prepared the cup
and its contents. They sat waiting for the water to boil.

In the silence of the early morning, I wondered if now was
a good time to broach the subject. It was Christmas morning
after all. Even Ebeneezer Scrooge had experienced a change of
heart on Christmas morning. Maybe a little of the Christmas
spirit had rubbed off on Daddy. So far, his mood seemed pleasant enough. There were no other distractions. It seemed as if
now was as good a time as any. I might as well give it my best
shot.

I had dreaded this moment for the past several days. But, it
was simply unavoidable if I expected to realize my dream of
spending Christmas in Paris. My unfortunate situation
involved a temporary, yet untimely, lack of transportation.

My '71 Buick Century had died on me about two weeks
earlier, just before my finals began. The end of the first semester of my junior year in college meant I was running short on
both time and money. A classmate helped me tow the car to a
local mechanic there in Murray, Kentucky. I explained my situation. I needed to get the car fixed, but I couldn't pay for it
until after the spring semester started in mid-January. (I had
already planned my semi-annual visit to my local banker
during the Christmas break.)

Apparently, this understanding mechanic had prior experience with other destitute Murray State students like me. He
agreed to keep the car at his shop until after the New Year
holiday, at which time he would make the necessary repairs.
He assured me that I could pay him and pick the car up after
classes resumed in mid-January.

With those details complete, I turned my attention to finals.
Within a couple of hours of finishing my last final, I had
hitched a ride and was headed back to Princeton for the
holidays. Since that time, for the last two weeks, I had been
immobile. Transportationally deprived, you might say. Totally
at the mercy of family and friends.

But, immobility was not acceptable today. Today was different. I <u>had</u> to have a car today. I just had to. There was a brown-eyed brunette expecting me to join her and her family for their family Christmas dinner.

Where was this dinner to be held? Paris. Paris, Tennessee, that is, eighty-five miles south of Princeton, Kentucky.

Normally, I wouldn't have made such a commitment. It ran contrary to my own rules of social engagement.

Van Hooser's Dating Rule # 7:
Never date anyone who lives more than
a dollar's worth of gas away!
(Exception: Rule # 7 can be ignored,
if your date pays for the gas.)

Down deep, I somehow knew that this was just too much of a hassle. But, young love being such as it was, I allowed romance to temporarily cloud my better judgement. I didn't pause to factor in common sense. Therefore, with blinders on, I dove in any way.

"Daddy, what are ya gonna do today?" I asked innocently.

"I don't reckon I'll do much. It's Christmas. I'm gonna hafta run down to the farm later and check the cattle, but that's about it. Why?"

Here goes nothing.

"I was wonderin' if I could borrow the car today?"

"What for?" he asked, as he cocked his head and looked my way.

"Well, I was plannin' to run down to Paris for a little while this mornin'."

"Paris? Paris, Tennessee? Why ya goin' all the way down there?"

"Well, I met this girl and she invited me..." I let my voice trail off as I watched his reaction.

Immediately, Daddy's body stiffened as he sat straighter in his chair. His gaze left me and was redirected to a spot some-where straight in front of him. He shook his head ever so slightly back and forth. I could tell this was not going well.

"Some little gal, huh? Well, I don't think ya need to go all the way down to Tennessee to see some little gal. Besides, ya can never tell what the weather may do."

It was unmistakably obvious that his mind was made up. I knew him too well. But, on the other hand, as I suspected he would, he left me one final opening. The weather. I knew he would bring it up. He always did. And this time I was ready.

"Daddy, I'll be back before dark and as far as the weather is concerned, I checked the forecast in the paper a while ago and they say it's gonna be pretty all day long."

His gaze returned quickly to me. He stared at me hard. Now he understood what I was doing on the porch a little earlier. He was on to my little game.

"You can't borrow my truck and that's that," he said flatly. "You'll hafta talk to your momma about her car." End of discussion.

I knew when to leave well enough alone. There was no sense stirring him up any more. Though the prospects didn't look particularly hopeful, maybe Mom would be more understanding. It was worth one more try.

I poured the boiling coffee water into the cup and delivered the cup to the table where I sat it down beside him. He didn't speak. I went upstairs to change clothes.

A little later, shortly after finishing a Christmas morning breakfast of sausage, eggs and Mom's wonderful homemade biscuits, I cornered Mom.

"Mom, can I borrow your car today?" I asked directly. I suspected that she knew the question was coming, even though I was sure Daddy hadn't prepped her. It wasn't his style.

"What for?" she asked.

"I've always wanted to spend Christmas in Paris," I said playfully.

She just rolled her eyes.

"Oh, come on, Mom. Whatta ya say?"

"I don't think it's such a good idea. Not on Christmas Day. Why don't ya just stick around here?"

"Mom, I really wanna go down to Paris," I said more seriously. "Just lemme borrow your car for a few hours. Okay?"

"What did your daddy say?" she asked.

"He said to talk to you."

She hesitated. Finally, she said, "Well, okay. But, I want ya to have the car home before dark."

"It's a deal," I said excitedly as I gave her a big hug.

In less than ten minutes, I was in the car, headed for Paris.

The drive to Paris took a little more than an hour and a half. The weather was beautiful, so the drive was pleasant. The first hour constituted the portion of the drive I was most familiar with. I had driven to Murray dozens of times over the past two and a half years. I knew virtually, to the minute, how long the fifty-five mile trip would take. Then, from Murray, the twenty-three mile trip further south down Highway 641 took me another half hour. Finally, I traveled through Paris, onward to the southern reaches of Henry County for my waiting dinner engagement. The trip was uneventful, with little traffic on the roads.

I arrived in Paris shortly after noon. After surviving the first few uncomfortable minutes of family introductions, and the inescapable "let's size him up" phase, I settled comfortably into the day's holiday festivities.

The dinner started a little later than I had been led to expect. However, even though I was dining with virtual strangers, the experience proved to be enjoyable. In fact, before I knew it, the day had quickly slipped away. I had done a poor job of watching the clock. As a result, there was no way that I would be able to get home before dark. I had to fall back to Plan B. I decided to head for home, then wherever I was when the sun started to set, I would find a pay phone and call Mom to let her know my whereabouts. I didn't want to worry them unnecessarily.

I offered my goodbyes and polite thanks for the dinner invitation. Soon, I was once again behind the wheel of Mom's Pontiac Catalina, settling in for the ride home.

As I made my way north out of Paris and Henry County, I was especially glad to see how deserted the roadways were. There was virtually no traffic. That would help me make even better time going home, I reasoned. Apparently, everybody was already where they intended to be for the evening. Everybody but me of course, but that was a temporary condition. I would be home in a little while. Or so I thought.

I was about fifteen miles north of Paris when the sun dipped behind the trees.

"Another eight miles and I'll be in Murray," I thought. "I'll call Mom from there."

However, as soon as I turned on the car's headlights I knew something was wrong. I noticed the panel lights before me were uncommonly dim. I drove another mile or two as I tried to sort out the situation in my mind. However, new problems were surfacing by the minute. In addition to unexplained dimming lights, I could also feel the engine steadily losing power. My attempts to accelerate proved useless. Finally, the engine died completely just as I passed the sign announcing entry into Hazel, Kentucky. I literally coasted to a stop in front of the only service station in Hazel, which, as you might have guessed, was locked and deserted. Just like every other business in town, on Christmas night.

I climbed out of the car, confused and frustrated. I didn't know the cause of these automotive problems, but I knew I had to do something soon. Darkness was falling. I immediately set out to find a pay phone. The good news was I finally found the only pay phone in Hazel, Kentucky. The bad news was the only pay phone in Hazel, Kentucky, was missing a receiver. The steel cord dangled limply in the breeze.

That settled it. I had no other choice. I had to hitchhike. Because I was a few miles closer to Murray than to Paris, I headed north. I started out on my eight mile hike dressed only in jeans, tennis shoes, a short sleeved T-shirt and light jacket. As darkness fell around me, the temperature did likewise.

I had walked less than a mile, when I noticed a car's headlights in the distance. As they approached, I began walking backward with my right thumb uplifted. I saw the car slow as it drew closer, but then continue past me without stopping. Dejectedly, I turned and continued my forced hike. However, approximately one hundred yards further down the road, I saw the car's brake lights shine and watched as it came to a complete stop. Then I saw the telltale reverse lights illuminate and I watched with interest as the car traveled slowly backwards until it was along side of me. I leaned over slightly and looked into the window. There I saw the faint outlines of two young boys and a girl, all in the front seat. None of them could have been older than sixteen. The boy riding "shotgun" cracked the window ever so slightly and peeked out.

"What's your problem?" he asked suspiciously.

"Car trouble back in Hazel," I replied. "I'm trying to get to Murray so I can call a wrecker. I'd sure appreciate a ride."

"I don't know. We'll have to talk about it for a minute," he said, as he rolled the window up again.

Very few times in my life have I felt so helpless. I couldn't help but think of Daddy's words from earlier in the day, "I don't think ya need to go all the way down to Tennessee to see some little gal." But, I ignored his advice and went anyway. Ironically, as I stood beside that car I was certain that, at some point in the past, at least one of these teenager's fathers had warned them about picking up strange hitchhikers. Yet, I stood hoping against hope that they, too, would ignore that good advice just this once.

Besides feeling helpless, I must have looked pitiful, too, because when the boy rolled down his window the second time, he simply said, "Get in before ya freeze to death." Even though I didn't know it before, apparently, some angels have pimples, drive beat up Chevy's and have no where to be on Christmas night. And, boy, am I thankful for them!

My rescuers drove me on into Murray and took me to Bruce and Sherry Francis' house. Bruce and Sherry, both native Princetonians, lived and worked in Murray. Though eight years older than me, I knew Bruce well. For several seasons we had played together on summer baseball and softball teams. We had already agreed that I would rent the upstairs apartment that Bruce and Sherry had available over their house when the new semester got under way. I was praying that they were at home.

As I directed my young chauffeurs to the Francis' house, I was thrilled to see lights shining through the front windows. I thanked the teenagers and offered to pay them for their trouble. To my surprise, and delight, they refused to accept any payment. They simply wouldn't hear of it. Their Christmas present to me they said, as we said our goodbyes. I appreciated their generosity. Besides, I only had eight dollars and some change to my name.

I knocked on the door of the house. Soon, I saw a face encircled by strawberry blonde hair, peek through the curtains covering the window in the door. It was Sherry. She stared hard for a long minute before recognizing me. By that time Bruce had joined her and opened the door.

"Phil, what the heck are ya doin' here? Come on in," Bruce said gregariously.

Before stepping into the house, I turned and waved one last time at the teenagers who had offered to wait and see me inside safely. They tooted the horn and sped away.

"Merry Christmas, guys," I began. "Sorry to barge in on ya like this, but I've had some car trouble south of town and I didn't know who else I could come to on Christmas night."

"Trouble? What kinda trouble?" Bruce asked.

"I don't know for sure. All I know is that Mom's dang car quit on me and it's sittin' on the side of the road in Hazel right now. If ya don't mind, I'm gonna call a wrecker and have 'em tow it over here 'til I can figure out whatta do next. Is that okay with y'all?"

They assured me that it was and we immediately went about the business of finding a wrecker service that worked holidays. Luckily, the first one we turned to in the yellow pages agreed to help me out. I was to ride with them to Hazel to retrieve the car. They assured me they would be right over. All there was to do was sit and wait. By now, it was well after dark.

"Phil, don't ya think ya oughta call your parents and let 'em know what's goin' on?" Sherry asked. "They may be worried."

Of course, she was right, they were probably already worried. But I couldn't call them yet. If I called now, before the car was recovered, they would be concerned that the car had not been taken care of appropriately. They would think that I was not in control of the problem. They would probably consider coming to Murray in the middle of the night to straighten things out. I didn't want any of that. I was convinced that I could work this thing out. I got myself into this mess, I had to work myself out of it.

"Yeah, Sherry, I'll call 'em, but not 'til I get the car back over here."

Before long, the wrecker pulled into the driveway. I climbed into the cab. Within an hour, we were back, with the car sitting in Bruce and Sherry's driveway. I gave the wrecker driver a check for thirty-five dollars and thanked him sincerely. It was the only check I had with me. Stuffed in an isolated compartment in my billfold. Hidden away for just such an emergency. But it was the last one. Not that it mattered much. There was less than fifty dollars in my account <u>before</u> I wrote this one.

As the wrecker drove away, I climbed back into the front seat of the car, on the off chance that it might just start. I felt like I had to give it one more try before giving up for the night. As I expected, when I turned the key, nothing.

I went back in the house and took off my jacket. Sherry gave me something warm to drink. Both she and Bruce seemed especially cheery and upbeat. A stark contrast to my mood at the moment.

"Well, ya can relax now, Phil," Bruce said, "the worst of it's over. This thing will look better in the mornin'."

I just looked at him and shook my head. If only that were true. Bruce may have thought the worst was over, but I knew better. The worst wasn't over. The worst of it was just about to begin. I still had to call home and break the news.

"Do y'all have a phone I can use?" I asked.

"Use that one right there," Bruce said pointing to the one in the living room.

"Don't ya have one that's a little more private?" I pressed.

"Yeah, we've got one in the bedroom, but there's no sense in goin' in there. Ya won't bother us. Use this one and be sure to tell Barbara and Joe we said hello."

Honestly, I wasn't much concerned at the moment whether I would bother them or not. I knew this call could be rather unpleasant. But, I wasn't in any mood to argue or resist vigorously. If that's the way it has to be, so be it. I slowly dialed the number. It never had a chance to ring twice.

"Hello?" was Mom's anxious reply on the other end.

"Mom, it's me," I said softly.

"Phil, where are ya? I've been worried sick." Her words rushed out in a torrent.

"Mom, I'm fine, but there's a little problem."

"Problem? What kinda problem? Has there been an accident?"

In the background I heard my dad's angry voice. "Where is he?" he demanded.

"I don't know, Joe," she said testily, obviously directing her words to Daddy. I immediately sensed that my tardiness had already been a major topic of conversation before this call.

"Phil, what's the problem?" Mom asked again.

"Mom, the car quit on me just south of Murray. The reason I'm late callin' is that I've been with the wrecker, gettin' it towed in. I'm in Murray now at Bruce and Sherry Francis' house."

As I spoke their names, I glanced up at Bruce and Sherry. Both smiled broadly, obviously ignorant of the turmoil raging on the other end of the phone.

How I dreaded speaking these next words!

"Mom, I guess I need to talk to Daddy to see what he wants me to do next."

"Joe, Phil wants to talk to you," Mom said evenly, but with tension apparent in her voice.

"I don't have anything to say to him," I heard Daddy roar. "I told him not to go down there in the first place. Let him call and talk to that little gal, if he wants somebody to talk to. Just find out how to get to Bruce's house and tell him I'll be down there to get the car in the mornin'."

Daddy's reaction, unfortunately, was not a surprise to me. He could be extremely hardheaded. He had a quick temper and often, was just as quick to say exactly what was on his mind. Sometimes his words were careless. Sometimes his words were hurtful. Sometimes his words were hurtful because they were careless. I loved Daddy dearly, but there were times that I didn't like him very much. I was sorry that Mom had to bear the brunt of the frustration that he was feeling for me in the moment.

"Phil, your daddy says that he'll be down there in the mornin' to get the car."

"Yeah, I heard."

"Will you be awright there?" she asked with a mother's concern.

"Yeah, I'll be fine," I said. I shared directions to the Francis' house and hung up.

By this time, Bruce and Sherry had finally sensed the tension in the call.

"Phil, is everything okay?" Bruce asked.

"Yeah," I said simply, without going into details. "Do ya mind if I sleep on the couch tonight?"

The next morning, I was up with the sun again. While the rest of the house slept, I pulled on my coat and slipped quietly outside. I was sure it would be wasted effort, but I had to try one more time, to get the car started. I opened the door and slid in behind the wheel. As I looked up, the frost was so thick on the windshield that I couldn't see the hood of the car. Slowly, I eased the key into the ignition. I pumped the accelerator twice, as was my habit, and turned the key. The engine turned slowly once, then twice, then all of a sudden it hit and the engine fired. It started! To my amazement it started. I was ecstatic. Maybe it had just been the battery or something simple. Maybe it was fine now. In any event, it was running and I decided to just let it sit and idle for awhile.

In a few short minutes, I saw Bruce appear. Apparently, he had heard the car start. He seemed almost as excited about my good fortune as I was.

"What did ya do?" he asked.

"Nothin'. Just got in and it started."

"Well, it prob'ly was a weak battery," Bruce observed.

"I thought so myself. Whatever it was, I'm just gonna let it run for awhile. Maybe it'll charge some before Daddy gets down here."

My spirits soared with the continuing hum of the engine. I stood silently, listening and thinking, "It'll sure be a lot better to have the car runnin' than just sittin' when Daddy gets here. Maybe this day won't be so bad after all." Bruce's next words interrupted my thoughts.

"Phil, I'll tell ya what we oughta do. Let's go down to the restaurant and get some breakfast. We'll drive the car and we'll just let it run in the parkin' lot while we eat."

The idea unnerved me immediately. "I don't know if that's such a good idea. Mom said Daddy would be down here early this morning."

"Phil, you know that it takes an hour to drive here from Princeton. If they leave as early as seven o'clock, they won't be here 'til eight and it's only six-thirty now. Let's go get a cup of coffee at least."

As usual, Bruce was his positive, enthusiastic self. His logic was sound. Yet, for some reason, I was still hesitant. I thought for a couple of minutes longer. I couldn't imagine what might go wrong, so, I finally agreed. We climbed in and headed out.

As we drove, the car performed well. It ran fine. I didn't notice any of the problems that I had experienced just a few hours before.

At the restaurant, we pulled the car near the window where we could easily see the exhaust from the Catalina's tailpipe in the cold morning air. We took our seats near the window and ordered biscuits with gravy and coffee. For the next ten minutes or more, I kept a close eye on the exhaust. We finished our meal. Bruce assured and then reassured me that everything was fine. Nevertheless, I still felt unsettled as I continued to watch the exhaust.

Suddenly, I saw something. Rather, I saw nothing. No exhaust! I leapt from my seat and rushed out of the restaurant into the parking lot, not taking the time to explain. Sure enough, the engine had stopped. I quickly climbed behind the wheel and attempted to restart the engine. No luck! I cranked and cranked. Nothing! Just like the night before. I felt sick. I couldn't believe this was happening. Not again. Not now.

As I climbed out of the car, I looked up and saw an all too familiar, rust-colored Ford pickup coming across the parking lot. There was no question about it. It was my dad. He was headed straight toward us. Even from a distance of fifty yards, I could see his face and eyes. In the cab with him, I recognized my brother-in-law, Sam, my sister's husband.

The truck pulled up beside us and its two occupants climbed out. Sam looked at me and mumbled a "good mornin'." I appreciated his effort, but I just nodded back.

"What's the problem?" Daddy asked.

"It started a little while ago and it just now quit again," I offered.

For all practical purposes, Daddy ignored me and my response.

"Bruce, can we pull it back over to your house and work on it?" Daddy asked.

"Sure, Joe. No problem," Bruce answered, immediately recognizing the tension in the air.

Quickly, we hooked a chain to the car and then to the bumper of the truck. When both vehicles were ready, Daddy turned to Sam and said, "Sam, you drive the car. Bruce, you can ride in the truck with me."

Rather sheepishly, I crawled into the car with Sam. I didn't like the feeling. I don't remember talking much on the brief ride to Bruce's house.

For the next three hours or so, Sam worked diligently in the bitter cold to identify the problem. Besides conducting various diagnostic tests, he kept the battery continuously connected to a battery-recharging unit. During that entire period, no words were exchanged between my dad and me. Neither of us made the effort. Finally, Sam announced to Daddy that he believed the battery was "hot" enough to get the car back to Princeton.

Immediately, Daddy began preparing to leave. He thanked Bruce and Sherry for their help and told them that he was sorry for all the trouble we had caused them. Both assured him that it had been no trouble at all. Then Daddy turned his attention to Sam and me.

"Sam, do ya mind drivin' the car back?" Daddy asked.

"No, Joe, I don't mind," Sam replied softly.

"Okay, then I'll follow ya."

Then Daddy turned and spoke his first words of the morning to me.

"Boy, get in the truck with me," he said.

I looked him in the eye and said, "I ain't goin'."

Both Sam and Bruce looked a little startled. Daddy just stared at me.

"What?" he asked directly.

"I said I ain't goin' home. I'm stayin' here until I get *my* car fixed."

I turned to Bruce.

"Bruce, do ya mind if I go ahead and move into the upstairs apartment a little early?"

Awkwardly, as if stuck between a rock and a hard place, Bruce responded, "Uh, no, I don't mind. But, we haven't got the electricity turned on yet."

"That's awright. If I can borrow a couple of blankets, I'll be fine."

I turned again to Daddy.

"I'm stayin'," I said flatly.

He looked directly into my eyes and said, "Suits me."

With those words, he climbed into the Ford pickup, and he and Sam headed back to Princeton.

I slept in that unheated apartment for the next six nights. During that period, I spent my eight dollars frugally, buying several thirty-five cent cans of Campbell's Chicken Noodle Soup (which I ate cold), and not much else. In the meantime, I was able to get the mechanic to speed up work on my car, while at the same time agreeing to extend the period of time that he would allow me to pay for the work. When my car was finally repaired, on the seventh day, I returned to Princeton for what was left of the semester break.

Neither Daddy nor I ever spoke of this incident to each other again. Yet, I must admit that I've thought of it many times since. I've thought of it often because I believe it taught me several things.

First, it reminded me that Daddy was not perfect. He was a man. Capable of mistakes and overreaction like any other man. However, this single incident displayed a level of impatience and intolerance toward me that was hard to ignore. I never blamed him for how he felt. But I did resent how he reacted. His reaction resulted in pain and discomfort for a number of people.

Secondly, it taught me to be more thoughtful and self-sufficient. I was wrong to take their car that day, especially when it was obvious to me that both Mom and Dad had reservations about me doing so. I was selfish, thinking of my own petty wishes. From that day forth, I don't think I ever asked to borrow anything of significance from my dad. Not because I harbored any latent hostility toward him. Rather, there just always seemed to be another way, a better way, to accomplish my purposes.

Finally, I noticed after this little event, that my dad and I never had another serious quarrel. Frankly, I don't even remember any cross words being exchanged between us. Certainly there were things that we didn't agree on, but somehow they were determined by both of us to be unworthy of a battle. I don't know if such an attitude was coincidental, or a direct consequence of what both of us may have learned from this experience. I just don't know, though I long to understand these things.

What I do know is, that as memorable as it was, Christmas in Paris was no walk in the park.

———

"Even a mistake may turn out to be the one thing necessary for a worthwhile achievement."

JOAN L. CURCIO

11

I'm Gonna Run

Home. At last. He must have felt free again.

Daddy was a twenty-one year old veteran, fresh from serving Uncle Sam as a member of the United States Air Force. His period of military service had begun just a few short months after the conclusion of World War II. On the eighth of October, 1948, exactly three years after being sworn in, he successfully completed his military commitment. Determined to put his European experience in the rearview mirror, he headed back to Farmersville, Kentucky—home. It was time to get on with his life. Little did Daddy realize that within a few short months he would make a decision that would change his life forever. The decision may have been the best decision he ever made.

About a dozen miles or so from the Farmersville community, at the southern end of Caldwell County, lies the sleepy little town of Fredonia. Two or three miles outside of Fredonia, Hobart and Thelma Traylor raised their family on the farm from which they drew their livelihood.

Barbara Ellen Traylor was the fifth of six children born to the couple I would eventually know as "Papa" and "Momma." Barbara was the youngest of four daughters. The Traylor family's daily existence and social standing were very similar to most of the farming families in the area. Hard work. Manual labor. Long hours. Personal sacrifice. Basic subsistence. Simple pleasures.

By the fall of 1948, when fate brought Barbara Ellen Traylor and Joe Van Hooser together, Barbara had already proven herself to be bright, motivated and determined. A blossoming young woman, she had successfully struggled with and overcome more than her share of early personal challenges.

Born in February, 1933, during the heart of America's "Great Depression," her childhood was spartan at best. The family just didn't have much. Few farming families did. By necessity, farming families of the day became experts at making the most of what they had to work with. The problem of course, there simply wasn't much to work with. But, Barbara's personal struggles took an early, more ominous turn.

During Christmas, 1934, Barbara, not yet two years old, contracted one of the most frightening and debilitating diseases the world has ever known. Polio. Today, polio has been almost totally eradicated around the world by way of early inoculation. However, at the end of 1934, a preventative vaccine for this horrible disease did not exist. Its discovery and application were still more than two decades away.

Fortunately, young Barbara was one of the lucky ones. Her illness was detected early and treatment began immediately. With the help of basic medication and homespun therapy, Barbara began to battle back. Of course, she could not have done it alone. Due to both limited medical treatment facilities and economic necessity, Barbara's recuperation and rehabilitation took place at home.

Hour after hour, day after day, Barbara's mother and sisters, Margaret and Pansy, attended to her every need. Each took turns standing by her bedside, talking with her, consoling her, encouraging her, all the while constantly and vigorously massaging her weakened leg. As desperate as the situation seemed in those early days, eventually the consistent combination of love, effort, prayer and diligence began to pay off. Miraculously, the circulation and the strength slowly began to return to the afflicted limb.

Although rehabilitation was long and difficult, after eighteen months, Barbara's progress was sufficient to allow her to begin the process of re-learning to walk. Her progress continued. Before long, she appeared to be back on an even par, physically, with other children her age. Yet, Barbara had to pass one more test before her doctor would pronounce her completely healed.

During one of her routine checkups, the country doctor who had treated her throughout the ordeal led Barbara to the sidewalk outside his office. There he positioned her next to her older sister, Joyce. Joyce was healthy in every way. As they stood side by side, he gave them their instructions.

"Girls, when I say 'go,' I want y'all to race down this sidewalk as fast as ya can. Understand? Okay. On your mark. Get set. GO!"

They were off. When they finished the race a few seconds later, there was no doubt in the doctor's mind. He proudly and confidently declared his young patient completely healed. Where once there had been serious concern as to whether this little girl would ever be able to walk again, now all such fears were extinguished. She could run!

Barbara continued to run in other areas of her life. Bright and curious by nature, she loved the process of learning and was ready for her formal education to begin when she started first grade as a mere five year old. Though younger than the other students in her class, she did well from the start.

As the years of her formal education progressed, Barbara's above average intellect and effort began to show. It became obvious that Barbara was ahead of her class. Her intellectual capabilities enabled her to skip seventh grade entirely. Starting school as a five year old *and* leap-frogging seventh grade allowed Barbara Ellen Traylor to graduate from Fredonia High School, Class of '49, as a sixteen year old—two full years ahead of the other kids her age.

Unfortunately, for Barbara and many other bright young kids of the day, the college experience and higher education were too often available only to those who could afford it. Barbara's family could certainly not afford to finance her continuing education.

But, as fate would have it, as high school graduation neared, higher education was not a primary concern for Barbara. Her attention was not fixed on colleges and degrees. Instead, her attention was focused squarely on matters of the heart. You see, she was in love.

Puppy love? First love? Love at first sight? Probably, all of these could serve as appropriate descriptions of Barbara Traylor's state of heart. She preferred to describe it as love at first *fright*. Here's why.

In late October, 1948, less than a month after returning to Farmersville, his military obligation fulfilled, Joe Van Hooser was in the mood to socialize. He found himself at a community wide Halloween party held at the Fredonia High School. During the evening, he crossed paths with an appropriately costumed pretty, young, raven-haired girl. That girl? None other than Barbara Ellen Traylor. She noticed him, too.

There was some sort of immediate chemistry. A strong mutual attraction. They talked. They laughed. In January, 1949, they had their first date. In January, 1950, they ran off and were married. He was twenty-two. She was sixteen. Their union had begun early, but it had begun.

I never had the opportunity to ask my grandparents, Mom and Dad's parents, to comment on what they initially thought or how they felt about the marriage of their two kids. Were they surprised? Were they angry? Were they concerned? Were they supportive? I can easily imagine they were some of all of the above. No, I never knew how my grandparents handled such delicate communication with their children. But, if it's any indication at all, I remember very well how *my* parents handled the situation with me.

I was twenty-seven and on my own. Susan Alsobrook was twenty-one and finishing her senior year in college. I had been out of college for five years, had a pretty good job, was sufficiently independent and in love. Nevertheless, before I proposed to Susan, I felt some sort of unspoken obligation to inform Mom and Dad of my intentions to bring someone new into the family. The day before I was planning to propose, I sat them both down for an impromptu conversation in the kitchen of their home at 408 Cadiz Street.

As I struggled to choose my words carefully, both sat in

focused silence. They could sense I had something important to share with them. I was seldom at a loss for words. I'm sure they felt the nervousness I was working so hard to disguise.

"Well," I began, "I thought y'all oughta know that I'm plannin' to ask Susan to marry me tomorrow night."

I'm sure my words came as no huge surprise to either of them. After all, Susan and I had been dating for more than a year. I knew they liked and approved of her and her family. Yet, the announcement of my nuptial intentions was not met by the joyous shrieks and congratulatory hugs some might expect. Frankly, I didn't expect any. I knew them both too well.

For a long moment, we just sat and looked at each other in thoughtful silence. Daddy sat, head slightly lowered, cradling a coffee cup in his weathered hands. Mom looked directly at me, bottom lip quivering slightly, blinking back tears.

Today, I can imagine that in those few silent seconds, both of them reviewed quickly, the previous thirty-five years of their life. It's easy to imagine them remembering the excitement and anticipation of the early days of their life together. It's also easy to envision them reliving the struggles and difficulties that inevitably come while two people work to build a life, a family and a future together. Without question, they understood and could foresee many of the challenges that awaited Susan and me. Yet, they kept such thoughts to themselves. There were no speeches, no admonitions, no grand predictions. Just two questions. Two simple questions. One from each of them. Both spoken from the heart. Daddy offered his first.

"Boy," he said, pausing to be sure he had my full attention. "I just wanna know. Have ya got your runnin' around over with?"

His question left no room for confusion. No beating around the bush. He understood youth. He understood young men. He understood me. He sat quietly, waiting for my answer.

"Yes, sir," I responded evenly.

"Well, ya better have, if ya expect it to work."

That's it. In a few short words, he had communicated his

primary concern in a way that was both unmistakable and unforgettable. As silence once again overtook the room, he shifted his eyes back to his coffee cup. That was his signal. He was finished. He had said all he intended to say.

I turned my attention to Mom. She spoke next. Her question initially caught me by surprise, though it makes perfect sense to me now.

"Phil, I just want to ask ya one thing. Can ya live without Susan?"

"What a strange question," I thought to myself. Nevertheless, I looked at Mom and answered her question.

"Of course I *can* live without her," I said. Then I added, "But, I don't want to."

Daddy's words sprang forth from logical, unemotional pragmatism. He knew the importance of commitment for the marriage relationship and the potential devastation brought about by the lack of it. By way of his simple, yet profound question, he was quite successful in reminding me of the importance of my commitment.

Mom's words were every bit as important as Daddy's, but in a different way. They too spoke to the situation at hand, but from a different vantage point. Daddy was the pragmatist, Mom the romantic. Not the in-your-face type of romanticism some think of when reading some cheap romance novel. Mom was the type of romantic who understood that any lasting commitment must be anchored in love. She knew there are times in *any* relationship, probably *every* relationship, where the level of commitment wavers somewhat. But, if the relationship is rooted in love, there is always a reason to stick it out and make it work. That's what she believed. More importantly, that's what she had practiced since January, 1950, when she and Daddy exchanged their vows and began their life together.

Their life together changed and evolved over the years. It began like many other marriages of that era. Daddy was the husband, the father, the head of the house, the bread-winner.

Mom was the wife, the mother, the helpmate, the homemaker. Today, many people make a special effort to go out of their way to question, challenge and even discount the legitimacy and division of authority related to this type of relationship. However, I would simply remind those people that this approach has worked for others. And it worked for my mom and dad. They were partners. Both committed and working to make the family work.

But, I said their relationship and their individual roles evolved over time, and they did. Mom faced many personal challenges and never ran from any of them. Over an eighteen year period of time, Mom bore four children. Ellen, the oldest, started college the year Dan, the youngest, was born. At various times, Mom worked in a variety of jobs to make household budgetary ends meet, or to provide for specific family needs that Daddy's paycheck would not cover. She worked as a factory worker on a production line. She performed basic clerical duties stuffing envelopes. She was an accomplished seamstress, sewing "piece work" baby garments in a hosiery mill, while doing custom sewing for individual paying customers on the side. She proved herself to be an accomplished salesperson, selling everything from ladies wear to shoes to baby furniture. Simply put, she did what she had to do, when she had to do it.

In early 1970, Barbara Van Hooser came face to face with one of her most daunting challenges. In March of that year, Daddy had his first serious heart attack. (Several others were to follow in the years to come.) The first was so severe and caused so much irreversible damage, that by June of 1971, Daddy had been declared permanently disabled. He was forty-three years old. His ability to earn a living in his chosen field, construction painting, forever gone.

It was a difficult and uncertain time for our family. Besides the obvious concerns we all harbored for Daddy and his questionable health, there was also the issue of income. All three of us boys were still at home (ages two to thirteen), while Ellen was away beginning her final year in college. How would we manage? That question weighed heavily on Mom's mind.

Soon after Daddy's first heart attack, Mom, anticipating the worst, acted. She knew she needed to find a job with good earning potential and scheduling flexibility. Oh yeah, she needed it right away. Her prayers were answered when, in the summer of 1970, Mom went to work for Field Enterprises selling World Book Encyclopedias door-to-door.

Like every other challenge she had ever undertaken, she approached her new job by running full speed ahead. It was the only speed she knew. She worked hard, learned quickly and sold plenty. During her first six years with the company, she realized a great deal of success. She earned awards, recognition, trips, promotions and most importantly, a solid income.

But, success came with a hefty price tag. Six years of running from one meeting to the next, one sales promotion to the next, one door to the next. Six years of running from teachers meetings, to ballgames, to doctors appointments. Six years of work and worry had taken their toll. Mom was physically and emotionally spent. We all could have understood if she had chosen to give up. It's easy to slow down. Easy to quit. But, she didn't. She couldn't. Her commitment, anchored in love for her family, wouldn't let her. Instead, she decided there was a better way. She decided it was time for a change. She convened a family meeting. She disguised it as dinner.

As we assembled ourselves around the kitchen table, Mom and Ellen hastily attended to the final details of the meal. I always enjoyed the times when we all gathered for a pre-arranged meal. Mom was an excellent "country cook." Meat and potatoes, corn and beans. Cornbread. Blackberry cobbler. Everything cooked in fried meat grease. These meals were always worth making time for. But, the food was just the beginning. The meals also allowed for conversation, laughter and a general sense of chaos I had come to expect and relish.

Unfortunately, by January 1977, these gatherings were happening less and less frequently. We were all off doing our own thing. Ellen was married and teaching school. She and her husband, Sam, were busy raising their son, Grant, and were expecting a second child in the summer. Both Mark and I were at college, leaving Dan, the youngest at home. Because of so many varied activities, we had seen less and less of each other in recent months.

As we settled into the meal, sporadic conversation was set against a background of clinking knives and forks. At the appropriate time, Mom broached the subject that I quickly realized was the central reason for this meal.

"Kids, your daddy and I have something to tell ya. I'm thinkin' about changin' jobs."

Her words had their intended effect. Immediately, we all sat a little more still and listened a littler more closely. She continued. "All of y'all know that I've gotten a little burned out bein' on the road sellin' every day. Well, your daddy and I have talked it over and we've decided it's time to do something about it. I'm gonna change jobs."

"What are ya gonna do?" someone asked quickly.

Her answer rocked us all.

"I'm gonna run for office," she said confidently.

I couldn't believe my ears. I had no idea what she might be considering, but never would I have imagined that she was considering running for elected office. Oh, she had always been interested in local politics. She and Daddy both had. But, never had I heard them, even remotely, entertain the possibility of getting actively and personally involved. I was dumbstruck.

I wanted to be supportive, I really did. Heaven knows that Mom had been a consistent encourager to me on almost every hair-brained idea I had ever hatched. She would always say things like, "Well, if ya really think it's a good idea..." or "Well, I'm sure ya can do it if you're willin' to work hard enough." Now I sat here wondering if I could find it within myself to encourage her.

"Mom, that's great," I think I said half-heartedly, hoping my words sounded more encouraging than they were.

"What office are ya thinkin' about runnin' for?"

"I'm gonna run for County Clerk."

"Which one is that?" I asked innocently.

"John Morgan's office," she stated flatly.

I almost lost my breath. John Morgan's office? Is she nuts? I didn't know much, but I knew enough to realize John Morgan had been in office for almost twenty-eight years. He had been in office since before I was born. He had occupied the office for so long, he had become emotionally connected with it in the minds of many citizens. For many Caldwell Countians, over time, the line had blurred as to where the office stopped and the office holder started. For me, and I'm sure many others, it had always been, "John Morgan's office."

And Mr. Morgan had done an acceptable job while in office. Most local voters liked him. As proof of that fact, Mr. Morgan's political affiliation was aligned with the minority party in our county. Yet, he regularly was re-elected by a majority of voters *outside* his party. Now, here Mom has announced her intentions to challenge him, in the first political campaign of her life. As you might imagine, I had my doubts. I think we all did. But, as I listened to her explain her reasoning for getting involved, I heard her saying familiar things like, "I really think it's a good idea…" and "I really think I can do it if I work hard enough." She wasn't overly intimidated by the task before her. After all, as she explained it, she wasn't "runnin' against John Morgan," she was "runnin' for the office." In her mind, it was fairly simple. I could tell she was committed.

In January, 1977, Mom took a leave of absence from selling encyclopedias so that she might focus clearly on the task at hand. The next day, she began the process of running her first political campaign. For her to even have a shot at unseating John Morgan in the general election to be held in November, she had to first win her party's primary election which would be held in May—four short months away!

One of Mom's first undertakings was to secure a map of Caldwell County—a detailed map that listed all the roads throughout the county. Once secured, the map was posted prominently in the house. Next, Mom would set out early each morning on her treks around the county. She was not out soliciting contributions. No one would offer any. She was not out making speeches to local clubs and organizations. No one invited her.

Instead, she walked and drove throughout the county knocking on doors, introducing herself to her fellow Caldwell Countians and asking them for their vote. Some laughed at her. Some felt sorry for her. Some ridiculed her. Some wouldn't even answer the door when she knocked. It was hard, discouraging, often demoralizing work. Yet, she kept running.

Without fail, she would return home each evening, a day of campaigning behind her, and mark on her map exactly how far she had gotten that day. The point at which she had finished the day would serve as the starting point for the next day's labor. When she began the effort, there was little to be encouraged by. But she kept at it and by the time the primary election rolled around in May, she defeated her two opponents by a slim margin of one hundred and fifty-seven votes.

We were so proud of her. Many people throughout the county paused long enough to offer her a smattering of polite congratulations. They recognized she had been working hard and most Caldwell Countians could appreciate the value of hard work. Still, with few exceptions, few people actually believed Barbara Van Hooser could defeat John Morgan in the November election. Her victory may have provided an energizing boost, but most voters were certain the effects would be temporary. She would surely lose in the general election.

Yet, these sentiments seemed to have no observable effect on Mom. She continued her countywide campaign visits, with even more gusto than before. Gradually, the people she met and spoke with began to offer more than a polite smile and casual handshake. They started engaging in earnest conversation. Some offered her sincere wishes of good luck. Some even said they were behind her, supporting her. It seemed remotely possible that something good might happen yet.

The night of the November general election was one of the most exciting evenings of my life. Knowing how hard Mom had worked and how far she had come, not just in the campaign, but in life, filled me with a tremendous amount of pride. I desperately wanted her to win. But, I had concluded in my own mind that even if she lost, it would be impossible for her to be a loser. Long ago, I concluded it's possible to run (or work) for the right reasons *or* for the wrong reasons. To win *and* still be a loser. To lose *and* still be a winner. In my mind, Mom had run for the office for the right reason. She was running for the office, not against the man. Therefore, she was a winner either way.

But on that night, hard work paid off. Barbara Van Hooser's campaign trail labors carried her to the office of Caldwell County Clerk, the first woman to ever hold that office in our county. Her margin of victory? A mere twenty-two votes. She was sworn in and assumed her position on the second day of January, 1978. She held the position for sixteen years, being re-elected three consecutive times before losing her final campaign in 1993.

I have spent many hours thinking about the personal and professional journey that has marked the life of Barbara Traylor Van Hooser. If one word best characterizes her journey, I think it might be the word "running." She has been running her entire life. Much of the run has been seemingly uphill.

She has run against the ravages of polio—and won. She has run against overwhelming negative odds facing a lasting teenage marriage—and won. She has run against the societal and emotional pressures associated with unplanned role reversal from homemaker to breadwinner—and won. She has run against the political establishment—and won. And she will continue to run—and win. Why? She understands the process.

Barbara learned early in life what some never learn. She learned that every aspect of life itself is a race. The courses on which we run differ. Some are inherently more difficult than others. Many offer unexpected turns and difficult terrain. Yet, the race continues. Prizes in life are not necessarily awarded to those who run fastest, but more often, to those most willing to continue to run. Over time, a few recognize the greatest reward to be the desire to keep running, regardless of the circumstance. For me the lesson is unmistakably clear.

Okay. On your mark. Get set. GO!

"The victory is not always to the swift or strong.
The true winners just keep keeping on."
ANONYMOUS

12

Miss Sophie

I slowed for the intersection and then turned left off Chestnut Street. I noticed the flashing red lights immediately. My heart began to race. The ambulance, the source of the flashing lights, was parked directly in front of the Powell Building.

I quickly surveyed the surrounding scene. As strange as it might sound, I was actually hoping to see a car accident, or some other misadventure unfolding along the street. To my dismay, there was no such accident. No unusual activity. The street was quiet. I immediately feared the worst. Something must have happened to Miss Sophie.

Miss Sophie had been my neighbor across the hall since I moved into my apartment in the Powell Building three years earlier. I had moved to Berea, Kentucky from Princeton, to accept my first management position after graduating from college.

The move to Berea represented a significant step in my personal and professional journey. In essence, it served as my individual declaration of independence. At the time of my relocation to Berea, I had been out of college for just under five months. During that time, I had been working at a "make do" job in Princeton, while living at home with Mom and Dad.

Over the years, as the end of my formal schooling drew closer and closer, Daddy had joked many times about ceremonially "breaking my supper plate" as a gesture indicating his belief the time was fast approaching for one of his little birdies to leave the nest. The approach and humor were classic Joe Van Hooser. The symbolism—unmistakable.

In reality, I'm sure Mom and Dad didn't worry too much

about my long-term intentions. I was twenty-two years old. It was time for me to be out on my own, making my own way. My parents knew it. My brothers and sister knew it. My friends knew it. Most importantly, I knew it. However, taking the first step out of the nest can be difficult. For most of us, the unknown can be terribly frightening. To overcome such potentially debilitating fear, occasionally some sort of specific motivation, some catalyst, is necessary to set the process in motion. For me, the catalyst came in the form of a job offer.

Before landing my new job, Berea, Kentucky meant nothing to me. From my personal vantage point, it was just another insignificant spot on the map. Just another little rural, backroads town tucked away in the heart of my home state. I didn't choose Berea. In a way, Berea chose me. In accepting my new job, by default Berea became my new home. In those early days, I could never have imagined the valuable lessons I would learn from the people I would meet and the experiences I would have during my time there. One of those very special people was Miss Sophie.

I remember my first encounter with Miss Sophie very well. After accepting the job, I made a quick return trip to Berea for the sole purpose of securing permanent lodging. I needed someplace to live. I expected the process to be a fairly easy one. I was wrong. As I checked out the few available apartments in the area, I quickly realized there were three primary obstacles to be overcome: cost, availability and furnishings. Yes, furnishings. I suppose, at that point, I just assumed there would be furnished apartments on the market to accommodate the needs of people like me. People who had just finished four and a half years of college. People who owned absolutely no household goods. None! Not even so much as a sleeping bag. I needed a furnished apartment and I needed it soon. The prospects weren't looking too promising.

As my only day available for apartment hunting began to draw to an end, I was faced with the very real possibility of returning to Berea in less than two weeks to begin a job—with no place to live. I began to experience the onset of one of those uncomfortable gnawing sensations, deep in my stomach, often brought on by pressure, anxiety and a sense of desperation. Some might correctly identify it as a stress reaction.

As I frantically, but unsuccessfully, made call after call to apartment complexes in the area, I happened upon a local resident who suggested I check out the lodging possibilities in the Powell Building. Without hesitation, I called the phone number that had been given me, spoke with the building owner, and to my relief a tour of the building was hastily arranged. Within a few short minutes, I stood on the sidewalk facing the Powell Building.

The Powell Building was a prominent, two-story structure, which offered office and retail space on the ground floor and apartments above. Hoping to get a better look inside the building, I leaned forward, cupping my hands around my eyes and pressing my nose against the large glass windows. I peered into dark emptiness. Both of the rental spaces available on the ground floor were vacant and looked as if they had been for some time.

I said the building was prominent and it was. But not because of its architectural design or fanciful decor. On the contrary. The building was a standard, unimaginative post-World War II block design. Needing paint and some overall sprucing up, it was functional, not flashy. Its prominence was based more on its location than its physical grandeur.

Situated at the intersection of Chestnut and Boone Streets, it was easy to imagine how, at one time, it served as one of the prime commercial locations in downtown Berea. However, over time, most business and commerce had gradually abandoned the downtown area, relocating to more convenient, profitable locations a mile to the west of downtown near the interstate highway, or northeast a couple of miles near the newer strip shopping centers. As a result of this gradual professional exodus, many of the once proud downtown structures began to slowly fade and fall into various states of disrepair due to vacancy and lack of attention. The Powell Building served as a prime example.

As I began to survey the surrounding area, I noticed that located right next to the Powell Building, on the south side, was a dull, poorly lit convenience store and parking lot which accommodated shoppers from 7:00 a.m. until 11:00 p.m., seven days a week, three hundred and sixty-five days a year. Directly in front of the Powell Building, across Boone Street to the west, sat a self-serve gas station which doubled as a continual gathering spot for a collection of individuals drawn from the local population. To the north and east, sat a variety of small, independently owned and operated businesses, including a grocery store, an appliance shop, a finance company, several empty store fronts and the ever present downtown Methodist and Baptist churches.

As I stood soaking in the scene around me, traffic flowed steadily past, all the while producing the inevitable sounds of horns honking, motors revving and tires squealing. The majority of motorists pausing downtown only long enough to obey the colored instructions—stop, go, yield—emitted by the stop light in the middle of the intersection.

Suddenly, a man appeared on the sidewalk from somewhere around the corner of the building.

"Phillip Van Hooser?" he asked.

"Yes," I replied.

"Well, I own this building. Ya called me a little while ago about an apartment. I guess you're still interested or ya wouldn't be here."

"Yeah, I sure am," I replied anxiously. "I'll be startin' work here in town a week from this comin' Monday, and I need a place to live. Ya got anything available?"

"As a matter of fact, I do. There are only six apartments in this building. Five of 'em are occupied. Three of 'em by the folks who've lived here for twenty-five years or longer. Mr. Powell and his wife live in the downstairs apartment on the back. He's lived here for as long as anybody can remember.

Upstairs, at the back of the building, there's a nice retired lady. Grace is her name. She's been in her apartment for more than twenty-five years. Then up in the front of the building, across the hall from the apartment I'm gonna show you, is where Miss Sophie lives. She's Grace's momma. She's lived in the building ever bit as long as Grace has."

"If her daughter is retired, she must be gettin' on up there. How old is she?" I asked.

"Ninety-some-odd years old," he said. "But she's sharp as a tack. She cooks, cleans and shops for herself. She's self-sufficient and just as sweet as she can be. Come on up. If her door's open, I'll introduce ya to her."

As we stepped off the sidewalk through the front door of the building, I stood looking up a daunting set of stairs that led to the second floor. I couldn't help but wonder how a ninety-something could negotiate them. By the time we reached the top, I was breathing heavily.

The landlord motioned toward a closed door to our right.

"Looks like Miss Sophie's already turned in for the evenin'," the landlord said. "Anyway, here's the apartment. Come on in and have a look," he said, as he unlocked the door and led me in.

I entered the corner apartment. Its windows faced both north and west. The apartment consisted of three rooms and no air conditioning. The setting springtime sun streaming through the large windows made the rooms uncomfortably warm. Noticing my reaction to the room's temperature, the landlord walked directly to the windows and cranked them open in an effort to provide at least the appearance of the possibility of circulation. However, the open windows allowed more than just a breeze to enter. From the street below came the unobstructed sounds of traffic. From across the street at the gas station came a variety of shouts, whistles, blaring music and catcalls common to most predominantly male gathering spots.

To add one more noticeable distinction to the overall ambiance of the apartment, the stoplight at the corner of

Chestnut and Boone, only a few yards from the corner of the building, was bright enough to illuminate the apartment's "sitting" room with its never ending progression of green, yellow and red "mood lighting."

The contents of the apartment were very basic. There was a sitting room (couch, chair and table), bedroom (bed and dresser), kitchen (cabinets, refrigerator, stove and dining table with two chairs) and a bathroom (toilet and tub). For a shower, I was instructed, one had to venture halfway down the building's open hall, past other apartments, to a small closet-like space that had been converted into a community shower. The landlord assured me that it would be like having my own personal shower, since the elderly ladies in the building weren't too fond of using it. It seems they wanted more privacy. Wonder why?

This apartment was not my idea of a swinging bachelor's pad. Even for my unrefined tastes, it left a lot to be desired. But it did have three important things going for it. First, it was immediately available. Second, it had a sufficient collection of mismatched furniture. The third, and most enticing feature, was that it was cheap. It rented for one hundred and fifty dollars per month, which included all utilities. Roughly, five dollars per day! I seized the opportunity and sealed the deal with a check for my first month's rent.

"I'm sure you'll be quite comfortable here," the landlord said half-heartedly, as he took my check and handed me the key.

Though I heard his words, I somehow sensed he was much more interested in cashing my check than he was my personal comfort. I took the apartment key and told him I would be moving in a week from Sunday.

As I made the two hundred plus mile drive back to Princeton that evening, I was relieved. I convinced myself that I had done the right thing. I thought, "At least I have someplace to sleep. I'll start lookin' for a more suitable apartment as soon as I get back in town and settled in."

Ten days later, I was headed back to Berea. This time, I was coming to stay. As a result, the longer I drove and the closer I came to Berea, more and more thoughts rushed through my mind.

"Am I doing the right thing?"

"It seemed like a good idea a few weeks ago."

"Wasn't this what I went to college for?"

"I can't back out now."

"I wanted to be out on my own, didn't I?"

"Oh, I'm sure everything will be fine."

"What will everybody back home think?"

"I'll bet my neighbors will be nice."

Mile after mile, in the deepest, darkest compartments of my mind, I found myself alternating between temporarily paralyzing thoughts of self-doubt and insecurity, to soaring self-created reaffirmations of hope and expectation. This was my fourth trip to Berea in the past six weeks. The previous three had been marked by various levels of anticipation and excitement. But, this trip was proving to be different. Significantly different. A new job to be learned. A new home to be established. New friends to be made. I began to realize it all starts anew when I get to Berea.

With a very real sense of nervousness, I pulled into the empty parking space directly in front of the Powell Building and stopped the car. With me in the car, stacked rather carelessly in the back seat and trunk, were all my worldly possessions. Indispensable personal items such as my clothes, a black and white, nine inch television set, my baseball glove and racquetball racquet, an armful of towels, several other miscellaneous odds and ends, plus a few mismatched pots, pans, plates and plastic glasses, as well as two green and black paisley print sheets and matching pillow case that Mom had shoved through my car window as I drove off.

As I began assembling my first armload of possessions, I thought about my new neighbors. By now, I was sure all of the building's tenants were well aware that a new renter would be joining them. I was fairly confident the landlord had told them all about me. If so, I was sure they were a bit concerned. A young, single man, fresh out of college. I could imagine their initial thoughts, their perceptions. I could imagine them thinking the worst. I knew it was very important for me to make a good first impression.

As I reached the top of the stairs, I made a point of glancing toward Miss Sophie's door. The screened door was shut, but through it, I noticed the main door was open. Through the screened door I could see a braided throw rug in the middle of the floor, a television set across the room against the wall, a chair positioned beside the window which overlooked the convenience store parking lot and an empty rocking chair sitting next to the door. But no Miss Sophie.

I unlocked my door and took the load inside. With arms empty once again, I retreated down the stairs toward my car in search of another load. This time, on my second trip up the stairs, I casually glanced through the screen door of my neighbor's apartment and spotted an elderly lady now sitting in the rocking chair by the door, which just a couple of minutes earlier had been empty. It had to be Miss Sophie.

Realizing we never get a second chance to make a first impression, I paused just outside my new neighbor's door, less than four feet from where she continued to sit and rock. With the load still in my arms, I faced the lady, smiled and spoke.

"Hey. I'm your new neighbor, Phil. How ya doin'?"

The elderly lady just looked at me. Then without speaking, she slowly lifted her foot, placed it against the bottom of the door, and with authority, slammed the door shut.

I stood momentarily, in shock, staring at the closed door. "Just as sweet as she can be, huh?!" I thought. My first encounter with Miss Sophie had ended rather abruptly.

I never understood the reasoning behind Miss Sophie's initial reaction to me. I never felt inclined to ask her for an explanation and she apparently never felt inclined to offer one. However, I have since concluded that one of the primary advantages of getting older may be that older folks are not expected to provide an explanation for their every thought or action. As it relates to older people, we spend very little time wondering or worrying about "why he did this," or "why she said that," or whether or not we could explain that "look on her face." We simply assume "that's the way he or she is," and then we leave it at that.

What I do know is that Miss Sophie came to visit me the next afternoon. As if nothing happened the day before, she introduced herself and welcomed me to the building. I invited her in and we sat and talked. She asked about me, my family, my background and then she told me about hers. The conversation was pleasant. After one conversation, I experienced a change of heart. She was "just as sweet as she could be" after all.

In the days, weeks and months that followed, Miss Sophie and I had dozens of conversations, with topics ranging from religion and world events, to family matters and my new beard. (By the way, she didn't like it.) She was candid and engaging. She laughed easily and listened earnestly. She would surprise me every now and then with a home cooked meal and I would make myself available to run occasional errands for her. I got to know her children and when people visited me from "back home," I always took them across the hall to meet Miss Sophie. Over time, we grew to like, trust and respect each other. Despite a more than seventy year difference in age, the strongest of bonds eventually formed between us—true friendship.

That's why the lights from the ambulance concerned me so. That's why I caught myself hoping to find an automobile accident in front of my apartment building. That's why I hurriedly parked my car and headed for the Powell Building, though fearful of what I might find. I was concerned about my friend.

As I stepped off the sidewalk into the building, the commotion was immediately apparent. At the top of the stairwell stood a uniformed Emergency Medical Technician peering through Miss Sophie's door. From the apartment, I could hear an unsettling array of muffled conversations, moans and shouted instructions.

Desperate for more information, I bounded up the stairs. When I reached the top, I grabbed the young EMT's arm. He turned to face me.

"What's goin' on? Is Miss Sophie okay?" I asked, somewhat breathlessly.

"Are you a family member?" the EMT responded, coolly.

"No, I'm a friend. Is she okay?" I asked again.

"The old lady that lives here fell and now she's resisting treatment," he said, with a businesslike efficiency.

Before I could dig for more information, Grace, Miss Sophie's daughter who lived in the apartment down the hall, stepped out of the apartment.

"Oh, Phil, I'm so glad you're here," she said earnestly. "Ya gotta talk to Momma."

"Grace, what's wrong? What happened?" I asked.

"Momma was pickin' up around the apartment a while ago, and she lost her balance and fell. I don't know for sure what she hit, but the attendants think she may have bruised or broken a rib or two. Phil, ya need to talk to her."

"Talk to her? About what?" I asked.

"They wanna take her to the hospital for x-rays and she just won't hear of it. She's bein' stubborn. But, she'll listen to you. Please talk to her. Please tell her to cooperate."

"Grace, what makes ya think she'll listen to me?"

"She'll listen to ya because she trusts ya. Please, Phil, tell her to go have her ribs x-rayed."

I stood silently for a moment trying to think as quickly and clearly as possible. The thought of trying to talk a ninety-six year old into doing something she didn't want to do was not a pleasant one for me. What would I say? How would she react? Would it do any good? Meanwhile, Grace continued to be insistent.

"Ya will try, won't ya, Phil?" she asked hopefully.

Not being able to produce even one good reason why I couldn't or shouldn't, I agreed.

"Yeah, I'll try," I said, with a considerable amount of hesitancy and reservation.

As I walked into the room, I saw Miss Sophie seated on the front edge of the couch, leaning forward, moaning softly. Though obviously in pain, it was just as obvious she was still in control. Two or three medical technicians stood around the room, keeping their distance, frustrated by their patient's lack of cooperation. I had absolutely no idea how to begin such a conversation, so I opted for something that from all indications, was in short supply in the room. Humor.

"Hey, Miss Sophie," I said loudly and cheerfully, causing her to look up at me. "They told me ya took a fall. Ya haven't been drinkin' and dancin' again, have ya?"

The implication of the question was admittedly preposterous. First, anyone that knew Miss Sophie knew her to be a lifelong teetotaler. Secondly, it was fairly obvious to all of us that Miss Sophie had not graced a dance floor in decades. The sheer audacity of the comment seemed to catch everyone by surprise. A momentary hush fell over the room, while everyone, including me, tried to determine whether this statement and the flippant attitude it represented would be tolerated. We all paused just long enough to take our cue from Miss Sophie.

For a few fleeting seconds she looked slightly puzzled. But, then her reaction gave her away. Gingerly, Miss Sophie lifted her right hand from the knee on which it had been resting. Slowly, she placed her open palm over her eyes and forehead. Grinning, she shook her head, and chuckled ever so softly. It was obvious to all of us. She got it. It was a joke. A joke. The tension in the room eased noticeably with her reaction. I walked over and knelt down in front of her.

"Miss Sophie, how ya feelin'?"

"Oh, Phil, my side hurts."

"Well, if it hurts, don't ya think ya oughta go with these guys and let 'em check ya out?" I asked carefully.

She looked directly into my eyes.

"Phil, I'm an old woman. If I go to the hospital now, they'll wanna keep me there," she said softly.

"Only if they need to," I countered.

We both sat silently for several seconds as she considered my words and I thought about what I might say next. Eventually, she spoke.

"Phil, do ya really think I should go?"

"Miss Sophie, Grace thinks so. These medical guys think so. So, yes ma'am, I guess I think ya oughta go, too," I said.

With those simple words, Miss Sophie relented and agreed to be taken to the hospital. Working together, we all moved her down the steep stairs and into the waiting ambulance outside. Within minutes, she had been admitted to the local hospital for tests, observation and treatment.

I thought about Miss Sophie a lot that evening and in the days that followed. I thought about her grit and determination. I thought about her will and the mental toughness it took to keep all of us at bay until *she* had decided it was time to go to the hospital. I was confident, as a patient at the hospital, she would receive the best treatment available. I knew she was in good hands. I knew they would provide for her every need. What I didn't consider was how important it was that *she* have something to do!

I visited Miss Sophie the next afternoon in the hospital. In the three years I had known her, I had never seen her lying down before. She was always up and moving. Her long white hair, usually swept up in a neat bun on top of her head, was down around her neck and shoulders. It was painfully evident that her spirits were down.

"How ya doin'?" I asked.

"My ribs hurt," she said. "I'm real sore. They got me taped up real good, but they still won't lemme go home. They say they're afraid I'll hurt 'em again. I guess they just want me to lay here till my ribs get better."

Miss Sophie's ribs did heal. They did get better. But, unfortunately, she lay there too long. Long enough that she ultimately lost her strength and her will. She didn't *have* to get up. Because there was someone available to attend to her every need, to cook for her, to clean for her, to care for her personal hygiene needs, Miss Sophie eventually lost the motivation, the pride of independence, that had driven her for so long. In a sense, she lost her reason for living.

Miss Sophie never came home from that hospital stay. She grew weaker and weaker as she lay in that hospital bed day after day. Eventually, she was moved into an extended care facility where, after a few more months, she finally expired.

The loss of Miss Sophie touched me. She was my friend. Too quickly, she was gone. I missed her.

But, her loss also taught me. I believe completely that all of us wanted the very best of care for Miss Sophie. We wanted her to receive the best medical treatment, the best personal attention, the best healing environment. Therefore, we did what we thought was best for her. Yet, at the time, I didn't fully understand the importance, the psychological impact of personal independence, for Miss Sophie and for all of us.

For almost a full century, this remarkable woman had lived a life built on the foundation of thousands of decisions she made for herself. I'm sure, through the years, some of those decisions proved to be better than others. After all, her formal education was limited, her personal boundaries rather narrow. Yet, she knew herself. She knew who she was, what she wanted and where she was going. Today, thousands and thousands of individuals, with brilliant, highly trained minds remain unable to answer those three questions: who they are, what they want and where they are going.

Because of knowing Miss Sophie, I have focused more on knowing myself. I continuously consider the importance and value of independence and decision making. I am hesitant to relinquish control of either to others.

More importantly, I have come to realize the most valuable lessons for life can often be learned by watching and listening to those who have already lived them.

"When something becomes personal, it becomes important."
NIDO QUBEIN

Movin' On

"Let us endeavor to live so that, when we come to die even the undertaker is sorry."

MARK TWAIN

- **Wash My Hair**
- **Big Al**
- **One Final Wish**
- **Call Me First**

13

Wash My Hair

I was almost ready to leave for work that morning, when the phone began to ring. Slightly exasperated, I thought, "Who could be callin' at this time of the mornin'? They're gonna make me late for work." Nevertheless, I stepped across the room and picked up the receiver.

"Hello?"

"Hello, Phil?"

I recognized the voice immediately. It was a voice that had spoken to me thousands of times since as early as nine months before my birth. The voice belonged to my mother. Yes, I recognized the voice, but I also recognized the tone of voice. As she spoke those two simple words, I began to feel unsettled, even frightened. I could hear the level of pain and fear in her voice. It was unmistakable. But, the cause was still unknown.

"Mom, what's wrong?" was my immediate response.

"Oh, Phil, I'm sorry to startle ya," she said, as she sensed my level of concern and anticipation, "but, I had to call and let ya know. Your dad's in the hospital."

"In the hospital? What's wrong?"

"Phil, he's had a heart attack. The doctor's say it's a pretty bad one. He's not doing very well at all. I called ya as soon as the doctor let us know something. Phil, I think ya oughta come home."

Her message served to stun me temporarily. I wasn't surprised to hear that Daddy was in the hospital. He had struggled with heart problems for years, and we were well aware of his worsening condition. What was most uncomfortable though was the way Mom presented the message. I could tell she was really worried. I could hear the sense of urgency in her voice.

"Mom, I'll be leavin' here soon. Where is he?"

"Now, Phil, take it easy. He's in Hopkinsville, at Jennie Stuart Hospital. But there's no sense in gettin' in a huge hurry. When ya get there they prob'ly won't let ya see him right away, anyway. They've got him in CCU on restricted visitation. Only one family member at a time is allowed in the room and then for only five minutes or so every three hours. They won't even let me stay. Phil, just take your time. If ya need to go into work today, go ahead. But, do come as soon as ya can."

"Awright, Mom. Lemme see what I need to do. Thanks for callin'. I love you. And, tell Daddy I love him, too."

I hung up the phone. I already knew what I was going to do. Quickly, I packed my bags. I was already dressed for work, so I decided to wear what I had on. In less than ten minutes, the car was packed and I was headed for the plant.

As I drove across town to Hyster Company, the manufacturing plant where I worked, I began making mental notes of the things I needed to share with Jerry before I left. Jerry Brenda was the Industrial Relations Manager and my immediate supervisor. He had hired me just a few months following my graduation from Murray State. I could honestly say whatever I knew about human resources, he had taught me. I had watched and learned from him as both a man and a manager. He had earned my unrestricted trust and respect. I thought of him both as my mentor and my friend. I was sure he would understand my need to go.

I parked my car in the first available slot and walked briskly to the Personnel entrance. As I walked through the door into the Personnel Department, I saw Jerry working at his desk. I stepped directly to his office and stuck my head in.

"Jer, ya got a minute?"

"Sure, come on in," he said, as he eyed me over the rim of the day's first, of what would certainly be many, cups of coffee.

"Sorry I'm late," I said, acknowledging my tardiness.

"No problem. I figured somethin' had come up. What's

"Mom called this mornin' and told me that Daddy's in the hospital. It looks like he's had a fairly serious heart attack."

Before I could go on and without any further details being shared, Jerry interrupted.

"So, when are ya leavin', Phil?" he asked, sensing and responding to my pressing need before I could even verbalize it. His words and supportive attitude served to lighten my emotional load.

"In a little while, if I can."

"Of course you can. Ya gotta go be with your family. Just let me know what I need to do to cover your bases here."

For the next few minutes, we reviewed the calendar and discussed the status of various pending projects. Once the essential bases had been covered and we both felt he had a good handle on what I had going, I stood up and prepared to leave.

"Jerry, thanks again for..."

Before I could finish, Jerry interrupted again.

"Phil, go home and do what ya need to do, and stay as long as ya need to. Just gimme a call every now and then to let me know what's goin' on. Okay?"

"I promise," I said, as I headed for the door.

"One more thing, Phil. Tell Joe that he'll be in my prayers."

I just smiled, nodded and left.

Within minutes, I was in my car headed for Hopkinsville, Kentucky. I knew the drive to Hopkinsville from my current home in Berea, Kentucky, would take the better part of four and a half hours. There was really no easy way to get from one to the other. Berea sits about forty-five miles south of Lexington, Kentucky, just east of the Interstate 75 corridor. It lies nestled in the western foothills of the Appalachian Mountain chain that runs further southward to eastern Tennessee and points beyond.

Hopkinsville lies more than two hundred miles west of Berea. Its surrounding landscape is far from mountainous. "Hoptown," as it's known by the locals, is surrounded by beautifully rich and productive farmlands. From a historical perspective, its primary claim to fame is that Hopkinsville/ Christian County was the birthplace of Jefferson Davis, President of the Confederacy. For me, the history of the area was much more recent. Located twenty-six miles south of Princeton, I had spent many hours playing sports and socializing in the area with my buddies.

But, as I drove westward that morning, my thoughts were not on geography, topography or history. My thoughts were on my father lying, in serious condition, in that Hopkinsville hospital bed. In the solitude of that car, I had both reason and time to consider many things worthy of thought and contemplation.

One thing that consumed a substantial amount of my time during that day's journey was the very real possibility, even probability, of Daddy's premature death. It was certainly not the first time I had entertained such thoughts. Not by a long shot. You see, Daddy had been struggling with heart-related problems for more than fifteen years. Since his first described "round" with chest pain in the mid-1960's (he was in his late thirties at the time), his heart condition had gradually, but steadily, worsened. By the time he had reached his mid-forties, his condition had degraded to the point that he had become permanently disabled, unable to continue working in his primary profession as a construction painter. In 1974, he finally agreed to have open heart surgery, at that time still a relatively new surgical procedure, in hopes of slowing, not reversing, the continuing damage. The surgery was successful, yet as time passed, his condition became more uncertain. Eventually, it became more and more difficult for him to participate in even the most sedate activities. Walking for example.

As I drove those winding two lane highways that day, I revisited in my mind many, many occasions when Daddy, Mark and I would be at the farm together. As Mark and I engaged in any number of farm-related chores and activities, Daddy would frequently choose to wander around the property. If you asked him why, he always had logical reasons. It might have been to walk the fences to see if any limbs had fallen on them after a recent thunderstorm. Or maybe he was checking the status of the cattle's pasture. Sometimes he just wanted to see how bad the weeds and morning glories were in the tobacco patch.

He always had legitimate arguments prepared to explain his actions. But over time, I came to a different conclusion. I believe Daddy couldn't stand the thought of living within vaguely defined boundaries. As dangerous as certain physical activities might have been for him, and he certainly recognized the dangers, he always needed to know exactly what it was he *could* and *couldn't* do—what he was either capable or incapable of. At the time, some of us may have questioned the intelligence of such risky actions on his part. But I now believe that Joe Van Hooser was actually driven to constantly test the limits—his limits. But isn't that understandable? After all, to learn what one is truly capable of often requires us to occasionally go *past* our point of physical or mental capability. Of course, there were occasions when Daddy did that, too.

From experience, Mark and I had learned to keep a continual eye on Daddy, ever on the lookout for any detectable signs of physical distress. On a number of different occasions, after Daddy had wandered off and stayed gone too long to suit Mark or me, we would go searching for him, scarcely speaking, silently fearful of what we might find. More often than was comfortable, we would find him seated, or lying, on the ground, nitroglycerine tablets in hand, waiting off the painful, sobering effects of his most recent "hurtin' spell." Yes, the fear and possibility of Daddy's death were ever present.

But, I didn't just think of Daddy that day. I also thought of myself. Specifically, I thought of my relationship to my family. As miles stretched into hours, I drove and reflected on the fact that I was the only one of Mom and Dad's four kids who had chosen to live and work outside Caldwell County, away from "home." My Berea, Kentucky home was a five hour drive. Much too far to be actively involved in the day-to-day experi-

Much too far to be actively involved in the day-to-day experiences of family.

My personal plan had been a conscious one. As soon as I graduated from college, I had headed out, anxious to find my own place in life. It wasn't an attempt to escape. I never felt as if I was running *from* Princeton, Kentucky. I loved my hometown and my family and friends that lived there. But, I was definitely running *to* whatever life had in store for me. I was anxious to test my wings and make my own way. Much like Daddy, I was intent on discovering what I was truly capable of. Not as "Joe and Barbara's boy," but, on my own.

But, as I continued to drive and think, I began to feel an uncomfortable and unexpected sensation of guilt welling up inside of me. I began to think that in some ways my actions, as innocent as they were, had been extremely selfish. They could have easily been interpreted as ungrateful. It dawned on me that I had never taken the time to explain my true motivation to Mom or Dad. Or for that matter, I wasn't sure they really knew how much they meant to me.

I began to think of myself as some sort of modern day prodigal son. Not that I was involved in the type of "riotous living" described in the Bible story. But I certainly seemed to be as self-absorbed as was the Biblical prodigal—worrying more about me and my self interests than about family, friends and the culture that had been instrumental in forming my values, my beliefs, my very foundation.

Was I being too selfish? During times of sickness and suffering, trials and troubles, such as these, shouldn't I be immediately available? Isn't that what family is all about? Does my family think I don't care about them? Do they wonder if I still love them? Did my brothers and sister feel as if I had abandoned them and my responsibilities? These questions, as well as many others, weighed heavily on my mind as I traveled.

After more than four hours of worrying about Daddy and wallowing in self-pity, I arrived in Hopkinsville. Soon I was sitting in the parking lot of Jennie Stuart Hospital.

In her call, Mom had mentioned the CCU visiting hours were extremely limited and that hospital personnel were very strict in enforcing them. I hadn't even thought to ask what they were. Was I too early or too late? I'd just have to go in and find out.

I entered the hospital lobby and was soon directed toward the Cardiac Care Unit. As I made my way through the busy, sterile corridors, I began to wonder what I would say when I saw him. How would I react?

As I approached the CCU area, I saw a sign announcing the existence of a visitor's waiting room. I figured if any of my family were still at the hospital, I would probably find them there. As I stepped to the waiting room and looked in, on the wall, I noticed a lonely television, with flickering images from some mindless soap opera dancing upon its screen. Otherwise, the room was empty, without life. I began to sense that I was too late. Visiting hours must be over. But I had come too far to give up that easily. I wanted to see my dad. I needed to see my dad.

Slowly, I continued down the hallway and entered the CCU wing. I noticed the nurse's desk, shaped like a semi-circle, located in the middle of a room. As I quickly glanced around, I estimated there were about half a dozen rooms serviced from this one station. Due to the semi-circular design of the wing, each patient's room was an equal distance from the nurse's desk. Each room had a glass wall at its entry point, allowing visual observation when necessary, or so I supposed. Just inside the glass walls, hung ceiling to floor curtains. Unfortunately, all the curtains were drawn. It was impossible for me to determine exactly which room was Daddy's.

This area was eerily quiet. The only sounds to be heard were an occasional beep coming from one of the many sophisticated pieces of equipment used for monitoring the condition of patients, or some far off loud speaker beckoning some aspiring Dr. Kildare. Unlike other areas of the hospital I had just made my way through, there were no faint, muted moans and groans coming from the various rooms. Just total silence.

As I drew nearer to the nurse's station, I noticed one solitary nurse on duty. She was engrossed in the completion of some sort of documentation and apparently had not heard me approach.

"Um, excuse me," I said softly.

The nurse looked up at me from her seat. I quickly estimated that she was only a few years older than me.

"May I help you?" she asked very professionally.

"Yes, I'm here to visit a patient. Joe Van Hooser."

As I spoke, the nurse stood and faced me across the counter.

"Are you a member of the family?"

"Yes, I am."

"I'm sorry sir, but you just missed the family visiting period," she said as she walked around the counter and stood beside me. "It ended about twenty minutes ago. I'm sorry, but the next visitation period is not for another three hours."

I sensed a measure of genuine regret, even compassion in her voice. I was immediately encouraged.

"Maybe there's an opportunity here after all," I thought.

"Oh, no," I said, turning and exhaling deeply. I stood with my back to her and shook my bowed head.

"Is there something wrong?" she asked.

I turned back to face the nurse.

"Miss, I am Joe Van Hooser's son from California. I haven't seen or spoken to my father for quite some time. My mother called and told me of his condition. She encouraged me to do everything within my power to get here as quickly as I could to see him and make amends. I flew into Nashville from Los Angeles, but my flight was late arrivin'. For the last hour, I've been drivin' like a mad man to get here and now ya tell me that I've missed seein' him by twenty minutes. I really don't know if I can wait three hours. Miss, is there anything ya can do to help me see him, alone, for just a few minutes?" I asked, while looking hopefully into her eyes.

I don't suppose my spontaneous, improvised performance was worthy of an academy award, but it was pretty convincing. Of course, virtually nothing I told the nurse was true, and for that I felt a little guilty. However, my conscious was eased, knowing that I had done the wrong thing for the right reason. I did need to see him, and I was willing to stretch the truth a bit to make it happen. I was confident she wouldn't do anything that put her patient, my father, at unnecessary risk.

When I had finished speaking, she stood looking at me for several seconds. Finally, she spoke.

"This is very unusual. But, I'll check to see if he's still awake. If he is, I'll see if he feels strong enough to see you for a few minutes. However, if he's sleeping, I'm sorry, I just won't wake him. He needs his rest."

"Oh, I understand," I assured her. "Thank you for checking."

The nurse walked away from me toward one of the rooms with the drawn curtains. I followed closely, and stood listening at the door as she entered.

"Mr. Van Hooser," she whispered softly. "Mr. Van Hooser, are you asleep?"

I heard my dad offer some sort of muffled response.

"Mr. Van Hooser, your son from California is here to see you."

As I heard my lie repeated, I cringed.

"Do you feel like seeing him?"

Clearly, I heard Daddy's immediate response.

"Oh, that must be Phil. Tell him to come on in."

Hearing his words, I couldn't help but smile. Some might wonder how he could, so confidently, know that the mysterious "California" visitor was none other than his oldest son, Phil? The answer is simple. He knew it was me, because he knew me. Even though I didn't think about it at the time, maybe he understood me a little better than I knew.

The nurse stepped out and whispered to me, "You can sit with him until he goes to sleep. After that, you must leave."

"I understand," I said. "Thank you again."

As I entered the room, I saw all the monitors, wires and medical paraphernalia surrounding my dad's bed. But there in the midst of it I saw my dad lying, with a closed lip smile, shaking his head slightly.

"Hey, Daddy," I said, as I leaned over and kissed him on the forehead.

He cut his eyes up at me and said, "Boy, what kinda story did ya tell that little gal anyway?"

I just chuckled. "Daddy, I just did what I had to do."

"Well, she knew better than to not let ya in."

"Whatta ya mean?" I asked.

"Well, earlier this mornin', some little doctor come struttin' in here like a l'il ole banty rooster and run your momma out. He told her to leave because I needed my rest. She hadn't no more got down the hall, 'til here he comes in again, this time leadin' about a dozen kids who are tryin' to learn to be doctors. And he stands right here in the middle of this room and starts to give 'em a class, using me as the example. That just flew all over me. I got mad as the devil. So, I run ever one of 'em off. I told 'em if I was too tired to see my family, I was too tired to see a bunch of quacks. Especially their leader." He said sarcastically, as he chuckled softly. Then he added, "You shoulda seen 'em scatter when all the bells and whistles on these machines started going off in the middle of my little speech."

I just looked at him in amazement. We both laughed. Right then, in my heart, I knew he would make it through this setback. He still had fight. He still had spunk. He still had the will to live.

For the next three hours, I sat at his bedside and we talked. Father to son. Man to man.

During our time together, I felt compelled to ask him questions that I had never verbalized before. In spite of his weakened state, he seemed somehow energized by our time together. The conversation was honest, open and heartfelt. At one point, I asked the question that struck at the heart of my greatest concern.

"Daddy, do ya understand me?"

"Whatta ya mean, boy?"

"Well, it's important to me that you and Mom realize that our family really does mean a lot to me. I love you and Momma, Ellen, Mark and Dan dearly. But, I worry sometimes that y'all may think I don't care about ya 'cause I seemed so anxious to leave home. Now, I'm livin' clear across the state and I'm not around when somethin' like this happens..."

My words trailed off as my voice choked with emotion.

"Phil," my dad said quietly.

With that one simple word, my attention was immediately peaked. For as long as I could remember, Daddy had referred to me most often as "boy." I sometimes laughingly tell folks, that I didn't know my name was "Phil" until I was fifteen years old. But, it wasn't just me. "Boy" was Daddy's name of choice for my brothers, his grandson and virtually all of our male friends. Though some might think it derisive or demeaning, he never offered the word in any mocking fashion. If anything, he used the word as his term of endearment.

Yet, on those rare occasions when he would opt to use my given name, I had come to realize it usually meant one of two things: first, there was either some sort of problem that needed to be attended to, or secondly, there was a message of affection about to be communicated. On this occasion, I didn't know quite which of these to expect. I listened closely.

"Phil, ever since ya were a little boy, I think me and your momma knew that once ya got grown, you wouldn't stay around home. Ya always liked to run around too much. There were too many other things that interested ya. And we don't blame ya a bit. That's the way it oughta be. It's important that ya find what ya like and what you're good at. That's the main thing."

Those words were never recorded in the congressional record. They were not carved into the cornerstone of some marble monument. They are not studied in history classes around the country. But, on that day, for me personally, they were more valuable than the constitution and the bill of rights rolled into one. On that day, those words served as justification for my personal declaration of independence, as endorsed by *my* founding father. With those few simple words and the sentiment he used to express them, Daddy unknowingly validated my inner desire to test my capabilities and explore life. I realized that it was really okay to follow a path somewhat different than his.

The approval, support and encouragement I had received from both my parents throughout my early life had been critical in enabling me to reach a point of self-sufficiency. In the months and years that followed, I would discover this particular conversation with my father, on his sick bed, served as a pivotal point from which my personal journey from self-sufficiency to significance would continue.

In the quiet serenity of that hospital room, my father and I talked and talked, discussing with equal interest both important and trivial matters. On several occasions, the young nurse would come to the door to check the status of her patient. Each time, Daddy would casually wave her away with a mere flick of his fingers. The conversation continued.

Finally, almost three hours later, Mom arrived for the next scheduled visiting period. She was surprised to find Daddy and me together, and shocked to learn that we had been together for such a long time.

By now, it was obvious that Daddy was beginning to tire and I knew that he and Mom should have some time together alone. I prepared to leave.

"Daddy, I'll be back later," I said. "Is there anything I can get ya while I'm out?" I asked, not really expecting a specific request.

Daddy thought for a few seconds before answering.

"Yeah, there is one thing. Pick me up some baby shampoo. I want ya to wash my hair this evenin'."

I was shocked at the request.

"Do what?" I exclaimed.

"Boy, you heard me. Get some shampoo. My head is oily. I want ya to wash my hair."

Mom and I looked at each other—both of us surprised by the request. Finally, I just laughed and said something to the effect of, "Okay. Phil's Salon will soon be open for business."

That afternoon, I picked up the shampoo that Daddy had requested. Later that evening, in the privacy of his hospital room, I washed my dad's hair. I had never done such a thing before and he never asked for a repeat performance. Yet, the irony of the activity left an unmistakable impression on me.

Could this have been a pivotal point of transition in both our journeys? The shifting of a father and son's relationship and responsibilities? The son doing for his temporarily helpless father, what the father, in earlier times, had done for his temporarily helpless son.

Or, could this have been just one of those special moments in life that I was lucky enough to capture in my mind, due to a softened heart and an attentive ear? Whatever the case, it was a moment of physical and emotional connection. A moment that I will always hold dear.

"It is better to wear out than to rust out."
RICHARD CUMBERLAND

14

Big Al

Monday, October 26, 1987. A day of stark contrasts.

A day in which I grew a little and declined a little. A day that forced me to behave like a man and think like a child. A day that tested my hidden strength yet exposed my obvious vulnerability. A day that dawned bright, yet discouraging and concluded dark, yet hopeful. A day I will never forget.

Yet, it started like so many others.

The weather was gorgeous. As I drove west across Ocala on my way to work, the sun was already high in the sky. Its brightness offered both warmth and optimism to all in its path. The Florida sky was cloudless, with a beautiful blue color similar to that of a robin's egg. Unlike some Monday mornings, this one dawned with great promise for the week ahead. Without question, it was destined to be an extraordinary day.

As I drove to work, I began to mentally organize my day and prepare for the week. Besides my normal workweek activities and responsibilities as a Human Resources Manager, this week promised special challenges. In just a few short hours, my wife, Susan, would be leaving for an extended business trip to Atlanta. Her absence would leave me with complete parental responsibilities for our six month old child. The thought made me slightly nervous. Could I do it? Could we manage without Mom? "Of course we could!" I reassured myself. But I was certain it would be a challenge.

As I made my way from the parking lot to my office, the folks I encountered seemed to be in an especially cheery mood. Everyone seemed to be having the same kind of morning I was. Maybe it was the full realization that, at long last, the late summer heat and humidity of central Florida had finally dissipated for a few glorious months. Maybe it was the afterglow of the company outing to the Tampa Bay Buccaneers versus Chicago Bears football game I had organized just one day earlier. Whatever it was, it was good.

Once in my office, I immediately reached for my daily calendar. As I reviewed my schedule for the day, I noticed a weekly planning meeting with my boss, Chip Carstensen, was first on the agenda.

I had only worked with Chip for a few short months. Four to be exact. But, I had already grown to like and respect him immensely. A few years my senior, Chip had recruited me away from another local manufacturing company. In our short time together, I had already developed high hopes and expectations for the work that we would accomplish.

As I made my way down the hall to his office, I saw Chip enter the building.

"Am I too early? Do ya want me to let ya get settled before we meet?" I asked.

"No," he responded cheerfully. "Come on in. I'll be with you as soon as I get a cup of coffee." After unlocking his office door, he disappeared in search of a caffeine fix. I stepped into the office and settled in. Shortly, Chip reappeared.

"Hey, man. Great job yesterday," he began as he slid into his chair behind the desk. He was enthusiastic, but sincere. "Everybody seemed to have a great time at the game. It was a good morale booster. Thanks for your efforts."

I appreciated the encouragement.

"Thanks. The feedback has been good. Good comments and no major problems. Maybe we should consider doin' it again. The only negative I saw was that Tampa Bay lost again."

"Hey, take it easy on yourself, buddy. Remember, you're no miracle worker." We both laughed.

As the small talk subsided, we quickly transitioned into more substantive discussions. What issues were paramount for the coming week? What do we need to be planning for? Were there any surprises that we could anticipate? The workweek had officially begun.

As we worked, we were soon interrupted by the ringing telephone. Chip excused himself and picked up the receiver. I sat patiently waiting for the opportunity to continue our session. As I waited, I watched Chip as he sat without speaking, listening intently to the caller. As he listened, he looked straight ahead, seemingly staring at my chest from across his desk. His detached gaze was strange. Noticeably unusual. Eventually, his eyes inched upward until we sat looking directly at one another.

"Yeah, he's with me now," I finally heard Chip say to the caller. "Go ahead and put him through to this phone."

With those words, Chip stood and motioned for me to come around the desk and take his seat. Confused, I stood and moved toward him.

"Who is it?" I asked, as I took the telephone receiver from Chip. "It's your brother, Mark," Chip replied quickly, but quietly. His earlier enthusiasm no longer evident.

Before I even touched the phone, I noticed it. An aching hollowness, deep in the pit of my stomach. It was a similar feeling to the one that occurs when an individual is awakened, from a deep sleep, by some unexpected, late night caller. The same feeling that presents itself when one encounters situations causing uncertainty and fear. Something was wrong, terribly wrong. It had to be. I could feel it.

"Hello?" I could hear the anxiety in my voice.

"Hey, Phil. What's goin' on?" were his exact words to me.

Mark didn't *speak* the words as much as they escaped from him, like a slowly exhaled breath. The words were innocent enough, but like me, the anxiety in his voice was immediately apparent. This was more than a social call. Much more.

"Not much," I replied without conviction. "Just workin'. Mark, what's wrong?" The question spilled out quickly.

Mark paused ever so briefly before answering.

"Phil, Daddy died last night."

Immediately, I felt the air rush out of me. I felt dizzy and lightheaded. I sank into Chip's chair. I struggled for my next words.

"What?" I asked, confident I had heard correctly the first time.

"Daddy died last night," Mark repeated patiently.

I must admit, I wasn't particularly surprised by the words. In my darkest thoughts, I had imagined hearing them from many different people on many different occasions. But I had never imagined hearing them from Mark. I was surprised by my reaction. I simply wasn't ready to hear those words.

"How?" I mumbled feebly.

"We're sure it was a heart attack. Momma didn't notice anything out of the ordinary durin' the night. This mornin' when she got up, she left him in bed. She thought he was still sleepin'. Later when she called for him to get up, he didn't respond. She went back in the room and started to shake him. That's when she realized..." Mark's words trailed off temporarily. "Phil, he died in his sleep. Apparently, there wasn't any pain."

Mark seemed amazingly composed throughout his explanation. But, the shock and emotion temporarily overwhelmed me. The rest of that brief conversation with Mark has long since been discharged from my memory. I'm sure I told him I would call later and let them know about our travel plans back to Kentucky.

As I hung up from talking with Mark, Susan suddenly appeared in Chip's office. I learned later that Susan's mother in Princeton had somehow heard the news of Daddy's death earlier that morning. Good news travels fast in small towns. Bad news even faster. She immediately called Susan at work. Upon hearing the shocking news, Susan rushed to my office to console me. Together, in Chip's office, we embraced, cried and shared our grief. One of my great fears in life had been realized. Daddy was dead.

As numbing as our grief was, there was little time to dwell on it. There were travel plans to be made and details to be attended to. We needed to get back home. Within fifteen minutes of her arrival, I had sent Susan away to prepare for our unscheduled trip back to Kentucky. Once she was gone, I retreated to my office and its quiet solitude. I needed to be alone.

Isolated for the moment, from family, friends, coworkers and curious observers, I sat alone at my desk, desperately attempting to gather and organize my thoughts. One moment, everything seemed to be so together, so composed. The next moment, everything was suddenly happening at breakneck speed. The harder I tried to focus, the less I could.

My disjointed thoughts were abruptly interrupted by my ringing telephone.

"Don't answer it," I told myself. "Someone else can deal with whatever problem the call represents. I can't handle anymore right now."

I sat staring at the phone as it continued to ring. Once, twice...five times, six times...finally, I could stand it no longer.

"Hello, this is Phillip Van Hooser," I said, trying halfheartedly to manufacture the impression of professionalism.

"Hey buddy, this is Al."

The deep, resonant, solemn response coming from the telephone receiver surprised me initially. It was a voice I had not expected, but one I welcomed. The voice belonged to Alan Tompkins. Tompkins was a friend. A true friend. An old friend.

Our paths first crossed in the mid-sixties when, as grade schoolers, we both were aspiring stars on our respective Little League football teams. Al played fullback for the powerhouse Blues, while I struggled as a running back for the hapless Reds. Our respective teams, along with the Greens and the Golds, practiced each afternoon, in the outfield area of the V.F.W. baseball park. The Reds usually practiced in the area immediately behind second base, while Al and his Blues teammates worked out in right field. Several times, during each practice I would steal obvious glances, in an attempt to keep an eye on Tompkins.

It was easy to spot him. In fact, he was hard to miss. Besides being one of the biggest kids in the league, he had an aggravating habit of looking good in his uniform. That was not the case with the majority of us. Most of us were satisfied to make do with one of our father's tattered undershirts, worn as a jersey over our shoulder pads. Our choice of athletic footwear was even more interesting. A great number of us spent significant portions of our practices and games slipping and sliding around the field in an assortment of well-worn "Chuck Taylor Converse Allstar" tennis shoes, hush puppies, or even "street" shoes. One of my teammates, Barry Cotton, actually wore his pointy-toed cowboy boots to practice, for heaven's sake. We were a ragtag group, to say the least.

But not Tompkins. Tompkins actually looked like a football player. I was jealous. For instance, he always practiced in a *real* football jersey with a number emblazoned on both front and back. Besides the jersey, Tompkins also wore "real live cleats." The kind that actually left holes in the ground—or your arm. Not just regular cleats. No, they were "high tops," no less! One of the most famous professional players of that era sported high tops—Johnny Unitas. Who did this guy think he was anyway, Johnny U? As far as I was concerned, that settled it. I didn't like Tompkins' looks.

But, over time, not only did I get used to "his looks," we became fast friends. Throughout our junior high and high school years, we grew closer and closer. The escapades and high jinx we both engaged in were considerable. Our many shared experiences served to strengthen the bond between us. However, as close as two people might be, sometimes you just don't know what you can do for your friends when they are suffering.

During the latter part of our high school years, Al's father was diagnosed with a terminal disease. I liked Mr. Tompkins a lot. He could always be found hanging around the football field during and after football practices, offering all of us words of praise and encouragement. I can't imagine he ever missed even one of Al's games. He was friendly and outgoing. He had a great sense of humor. Unfortunately, while still in the prime of his life, he was facing the end. It must have been a terribly difficult time for the entire Tompkins' family. But because of our friendship, I thought and worried most about Al.

As the youngest of four children, Al and his father seemed to have a close personal relationship. However, throughout his father's illness, leading up to and following his death, Al and I never talked much about what was going on or how Al was coping. I was young and woefully inexperienced in such matters of life and death. I felt *sorry* for Al and his family, but somehow sympathy didn't seem to be enough. But it was all I had. I was hesitant, possibly overly cautious, about asking personal, probing questions. I wanted to be there for him, but I didn't want to make a difficult situation even more so for Al. As a result, Al seemed to suffer in silence. Though he had my sympathies, I know I was not much practical help or comfort. I didn't know how to be.

Following Mr. Tompkins' death, days passed to months and months to years. Al and I completed our high school experience and headed off for Murray State University. There we continued to build memories as roommates during our freshmen year.

Before the start of our sophomore year, Tompkins left Murray State and transferred to Western Kentucky University. There he actively pursued his personal dream of becoming a professional broadcaster.

In the years that followed college, both Al and I focused on our professional careers. As I explored opportunities in manufacturing management, Al began to realize his broadcasting dream. By October 26, 1987, he had become an award winning investigative reporter for the news division of WSMV-TV, Nashville, Tennessee's NBC affiliate station.

It had been quite a while since I had talked to Al. Now, just hearing his voice served to offer an encouraging feeling of calm stability during a time when it was needed most.

"Al, it's good to hear your voice," I began.

"Phil, I just heard about Joe. I want ya to know how sorry I am. I thought a lot of your dad."

And Daddy thought a lot of Al. I couldn't help but think of my dad's relationship with Tompkins. Daddy approved of, and got along well with most of my friends, but Tompkins was one of his obvious favorites. On many occasions, I have heard my Dad summarize his feelings for Tompkins by saying, "Al is a good ole boy." There was no higher praise that Daddy would, or could, heap on someone.

There were a number of things that appealed to Daddy about Tompkins. First, Daddy liked the fact that Tompkins had grown up on a farm and had labored in hay fields, tobacco patches and at one of the county's major hog farms. From Daddy's perspective, Tompkins was industrious, energetic and "a worker." Daddy liked that.

Secondly, Daddy appreciated Tompkins' continual inclination to always have some project working which held great promise for personal and financial reward. While engrossed in discussing such future opportunities, more often than not, they frittered away the present trading used pocketknives.

Finally, Daddy respected the fact that Tompkins would sit and talk when he came by the house, instead of just rushing off as soon as possible, in search of female companionship, or some other adventure which lay waiting at the Burger Queen or beyond. Tompkins always had a story that Daddy "needed to hear." Daddy, in turn, would gladly reciprocate. Their affection for one another was genuine.

"Thanks, Al," I said sincerely. "I appreciate ya callin'."

"Listen, Phil, I'm sorry to have to rush, but I've got a meeting I need to get to. How are ya plannin' to get home for the funeral?"

"We'll be flyin' into Nashville later tonight. I don't know exactly when yet. I'm gonna call my travel agent as soon as I get off the phone to make the arrangements."

"Will anybody be meeting ya at the airport?" Tompkins asked.

"No. I'm gonna rent a car and drive to Princeton."

"Don't rent a car," Al said flatly. "Call my office as soon as ya know your flight schedule and tell them when you'll be arrivin'. I'll meet ya at the airport and drive ya home. It's gonna be a long day, leave the drivin' to me."

I knew Tompkins. This was no hollow offer he hoped I would refuse.

"Are ya sure?" I asked. "It'll prob'ly be late."

"Just call. Be careful. I'll see ya tonight." With those parting words, he hung up.

The balance of the day was basically a blur. So much to be done, yet so many distractions, both physical and emotional, to complicate the process. By the time we finally boarded the airplane in Orlando, later that night, for the flight to Nashville, the burdens of the day were beginning to weigh heavier and heavier.

Our flight finally touched down in Nashville just before 10:00 p.m. As we taxied to the terminal, I wondered to myself if he would still be waiting. It was so late! I shouldn't have worried.

As we exited the plane and walked wearily up the jetway toward the gate area, I could see Al standing tall, waiting patiently for us. As we drew nearer, I saw a warm, familiar smile on his face. As we reached one another, I don't remember a lot of words being spoken. We shook hands and then embraced. Al hugged Susan and then turned his attention to our six month old. At that point, Tompkins presented a small, stuffed animal.

The picture of that scene remains securely etched in my mind. Big Al Tompkins, all six feet four inches of him, bending gently forward to present a twelve-inch, blue, stuffed teddy bear to our young son. Through sheer will, Tompkins had transformed an occasion forced on us by painful loss, into a brief, but joyful occasion for unselfish sharing.

We retrieved our luggage and soon, the four of us were tightly packed into the cab of Al's pickup truck for the one hundred and five mile drive through the darkness to Princeton.

As we turned onto Cadiz Street, off Highway 139, directly in front of the V.F.W. ballpark, the very spot where our friendship took root two decades earlier, 408 Cadiz Street soon came into sight. It was nearing midnight, yet lights burned brightly throughout the house. The truck's headlights illuminated the house as we turned left and pulled into the driveway. Before we could climb completely out of the truck, we were met in the yard by family members anticipating our arrival. There were the predictable hugs, kisses and tears. There was an understated joy knowing that the family was reunited, though the reunion itself was brought about by the sobering loss of the patriarch. But, strength was drawn from one another. We were stronger because we shared the experience together and with Al.

Al was greeted warmly and appreciatively by my mother, brothers and sister. In turn, Al expressed his heartfelt sympathies regarding our loss. But, when Mom invited him to come in the house and have something to eat, Al politely, but firmly, declined.

"No, I don't have time. I need to get back to Nashville. I've got to work in the morning. Just know that I'll be thinkin' of y'all during this difficult time."

With those simple words, Al was soon back in his truck, settling in for his two-hour trip, and his estimated 2:00 a.m. arrival back in Nashville.

I now understand there is a significant practical difference between *sympathy* and *empathy*.

Sympathy, I have come to believe, is the easier of the two. Sympathy is more distant and detached. Sympathy allows us to truly *feel sorry* for someone, but often without *doing* anything more. That was my situation, I'm sorry to say, as it related to the death of Mr. Tompkins. I felt sorry for Al. I felt sorry for the family. But, I did little else. Honestly, I didn't know what I could do.

Empathy, on the other hand, expects more of us. Empathy allows us the opportunity *to feel as others are feeling*. Once we learn to be sensitive to the real nature of another's pain and loss, we somehow begin to realize what others need from us. We recognize that human needs are often very basic in nature—a smile, a hug, an encouraging word or maybe even a ride from the airport.

I learned the difference between sympathy and empathy from a big man. A big man, with a little truck. A big man, with a little bear. A big man, with a little time. A big man, with a huge heart.

That man?

Big Al.

———

"Wherever you are, be all there."

CHUCK SWINDOLL

15

One Final Wish

Goodbyes are never easy. They always seem so final. However, with Daddy's death, we were all faced with the unenviable task of saying goodbye.

Once back in Princeton, back in the house at 408 Cadiz Street, the finality of Daddy's passing began to settle in. A mere twenty-four hours earlier, my father had walked the same floors that we now walked. All around were visible signs of his earthly existence. His clothes, his billfold, his watch, his chair, his comb. They all remained. Yet, he was gone. Gone forever.

Even more evident than Daddy's absence, was the stark reality of our continued presence. We remained. Together. Together to deal with the new realities of our irreversibly changed lives.

Together, but at the same time alone. Alone and heartbroken. Each of us left with the personal responsibility to manage the shock and grief brought on by the loss. Three of us were supported and comforted during this trying period by spouses. Only Mom and my youngest brother, Dan, were without the benefit of a helpmate to walk with them through this time of mourning.

Gradually, the night of Daddy's death gave way to the early morning hours of October 27, 1987. Though mentally, physically and emotionally drained, none of us seemed anxious to retire for the evening. Maybe we silently feared that sleep wouldn't come. The mere possibility that our night would be spent wrestling with the unanswerable questions that accompany unimaginable circumstances caused discomfort. Tonight, the quiet stillness of a darkened bedroom held no allure.

No, it seemed much better to fight off the urge to rest until physical exhaustion completely overtook us. We found a certain security that came with the knowledge of being surrounded by loved ones, though all were struggling with similar personal issues.

The dark, peaceful solitude of a new day found us scattered throughout the kitchen and dining room area of Mom and Dad's home. Thinking. Talking. Sometimes thinking without talking. Sometimes talking without thinking. Sometimes both, sometimes neither.

We all sat gathered around the same dining room table that had been ground zero for hundreds of family conversations in years past. Some monumental, some ridiculous.

Marriages and births had been discussed and anticipated here. Financial windfalls and pitfalls had been dissected and analyzed here. Personal problems and concerns had been displayed and announced here. Tonight was no different. This was where the business of family was conducted.

There were obvious questions for which all of us needed answers. For me, having not arrived home until more than sixteen hours following the discovery of my father's body, I was curious about many of the specific decisions that had already been made.

As Mom recounted the activities of the day for me, I was impressed by the apparent ease and forethought with which she had handled many of the troubling details involving the upcoming funeral service and burial. However, I soon learned that some of the details had been determined by Daddy himself long before. He had provided specific instructions that Mom was able to carry out with relative ease. The things important to him. The list of pallbearers. The preacher to lead the service. The burial plot. For each of these Daddy had carefully considered and communicated his wishes, in thoughtful anticipation of this eventual reality.

There were other issues to be attended to that could not have been anticipated. Issues unique to various members of the family. One I remember vividly concerned my younger brother, Dan.

Dan was determinedly insistent that the men of the family be the actual pallbearers. It was Dan's explicit desire that the casket be physically borne, from the funeral home to the cemetery, by the three sons (Dan, Mark and me), the son-in-law (Sam) and the oldest grandson (Grant). Dan was passionate in his desire. It was so decided. As a result, the list of men Daddy had intended as pallbearers served in an honorary capacity. I am confident Daddy would have been pleased with the unplanned departure from his original plans. Such was the nature of our family discussions in these pre-dawn hours.

As I sat listening and thinking throughout the evening, a thought returned to me that had crossed my mind several times during the hours since I had learned of Daddy's death. Finally, I decided to pose the question to my assembled family members. I realized it was strange and somewhat vague, but there was purpose in asking it. I hoped someone would appreciate the nature of the question.

"Have y'all thought about anything special that ya would like to have happen between now and the funeral?" I asked.

The question was directed to no one in particular, everyone in general. I looked around the room at the familiar faces as each considered my words. Initially, there was no response. Silence settled over the room. Eventually, someone spoke up.

"Phil, whatta ya mean?"

"I can't say for sure," I began, "but, since this mornin' I've been havin' the same thought. All of us know how much Daddy enjoyed goin' to the funeral home and tellin' stories. I guess I just wanna hear some stories about him. I'd love to hear a story from some of his old friends that I've never heard before. I wish I could hear some story about him that'd make me laugh."

There was no audible response to my question or comment. Yet, I was confident they were beginning to understand what I meant. I watched as some of those seated around me nodded their heads.

Growing up in a small, rural community, everybody knew,

or knew of, everybody else. Anonymity and isolation were virtually impossible. The simple act of daily living resulted in multiple and repeated intersections of various lives on many different fronts. Folks worked together, worshiped together and worried together—about taxes, the weather, the price of a gallon of milk, declining moral standards or any number of other common areas of concern. These were diverse individuals striving, sometimes struggling, together for a common purpose— "life, liberty and the pursuit of happiness." Over time, I came to realize that this shared commonality is the very fabric that knits a community together.

I learned early on that for close-knit communities, the passing of a family member or neighbor was much more than a brief period of mourning and grief. In a very real way, it was cause for a period of remembrance and celebration. Death provided a tangible opportunity to remember and celebrate the life and memory of the recently departed. But, it also served as an opportunity for the living to remember and celebrate the very nature of life, family, friends and community.

In generations as recent as my father's and grandfather's, when death visited a rural community, neighbors responded. Contrary to the old saying, "the size of a person's funeral is dependent solely on the weather," I heard the men and women of my mom and dad's generation share wonderful stories of neighbor helping neighbor. In Farmersville, Kentucky, when death occurred, the community would turn out in great numbers to do what needed to be done. These trying times were marked by simple acts of reverence and respect.

For example, before the widespread appearance of private funeral homes, the unenviable task of preparing the body of the deceased for burial was conducted by men throughout the community. Friends and neighbors. Once preparations were complete, the body of the recently deceased would be made available for "viewing." This period of communal mourning would be conducted at the departed's home, right up until time for the church funeral and cemetery burial. For two or more days, family, friends and neighbors alike would "sit up," or hold vigil, around the clock, at the home of the departed.

During this period of mourning, neighbors and friends would "pay their respects" in a number of ways. Calls and cards, visits and verses, flowers and food. Lots of food. All of it intended to satisfy the physical needs of those assembled. Heaping platters of fried chicken, pork chops and baked ham. Skillet after skillet of cornbread. Seemingly, endless bowls of vegetables, including green beans, baked beans, white beans, lima beans, pinto beans, black-eyed peas and stewed potatoes. Countertops crowded with cakes, pies and cobblers of the coconut, chocolate, apple, peach and blackberry varieties. All prepared and delivered *by* friends and loved ones, *to* friends and loved ones.

During my childhood, I watched as this cultural tradition of mourning at home was gradually, yet completely, abandoned for the more convenient method we practice today. Funeral homes secured their position as the appropriate place to publicly honor and mourn the deceased. Though the locations changed, the need to come together on such occasions remained. Out of obligation, respect and to some degree, a sense of habit, family, friends and neighbors still head to funeral homes for the purpose of paying their respect.

Though no longer necessary to sit up with the body around the clock, my parent's generation seemed in no big hurry to rush through the process. At the dozens and dozens of funeral home viewing occasions I have been witness to, the general rule has been that people *do not* simply file past the casket, offer a few words of condolence and then slip quickly and quietly away. More often than not, with the body of friend and neighbor positioned at the opposite end of the room, visitors seize the opportunity to fellowship and reminisce, often sharing candid personal stories and recollections of their past experiences with the recently departed.

It was during these times that Daddy may have been at his best. He loved stories. He loved to hear them. Better still, he loved to tell them. The exuberant laughter he personally shared during his stories, as well as the laughter his stories evoked, might have seemed, to some, out of place. Possibly even irreverent. But, that wasn't the case at all. As I recall it being explained to me early on, there is no sin in laughing at a funeral. After all, consider the first three letters of the word "funeral." They spell "fun."

That simple explanation was sufficient for me as a child. However, as an adult I have given the matter more serious consideration. As a result, I have come to the following conclusion. Genuine, heartfelt joy, as evidenced by laughter, can serve as an eternal memorial for all of us. The ability to recall the life and experiences of someone and laugh provides evidence that the person's life and existence somehow mattered. It mattered because it personally impacted another. It mattered because it brought joy. It mattered and therefore, is worth remembering. If something (or someone) was worth remembering, then certainly it was worth sharing with others. In a way, with the telling and retelling of these stories from life, a lasting legacy is being forged.

If I'm right, then in his own way, Daddy was a legacy builder. I often thought him capable, through his stories and sense of humor, of sending both mourners *and* the dearly departed away on their respective journeys with a smile on their faces.

Because of all of this, I wanted to hear a new story about Daddy. I needed something else, from someone else, to offer me assurance that Daddy's memory would be lasting. I needed to know that his legacy would be secure. But, I had no control over such things. The issues facing us were more immediate, more basic. The emotional challenges of the next forty-eight hours still loomed before us.

As our physical and emotional fatigue led us toward exhaustion, the dining room conversation began to dwindle. Eventually, we all slipped away in search of sleep and, hopefully, rest.

Morning came quickly, ushered in by phone calls and visitors. A flurry of activity overtook us as we went about our mental and physical preparations for the funeral home visitation. By mid-afternoon, the immediate family had reassembled at Mom's house in anticipation of the one mile journey to Morgan's Funeral Home for the private family viewing period. Public visitation would follow.

As final preparations were being made to leave the house, the tension was obvious, but unstated. I began to feel a sense of dread and uncertainty building within me. How would I react to seeing Daddy's body there? Would I be able to go through with it? Would I break down? What would the others think? There were so many questions. So many unanswered questions.

As we arrived at Morgan's Funeral Home at the predetermined time, we were met in the lobby by Ricky Morgan, the third generation of the Morgan family to manage the Princeton facility. I had known Ricky for years. Though a few years older than me, over the years a friendship had developed between us. I had always appreciated his sense of humor and easygoing manner. But today there was no laughter, no frivolous bantering. Ricky greeted us with compassion and professional courtesy. He assured us that everything was in order. He asked if we were ready to go in. It was a difficult moment.

As we walked down the hall, I could see through the opening leading into the viewing room. I noticed a large number of colorful floral arrangements lining the wall opposite the door through which we would soon enter. Daddy would have feigned disgust at the extravagance of the flowers, even though he and Mom had bought dozens of such arrangements for others. Nevertheless, I was confident he would have been pleased by the beautiful symbols of love and affection the flowers represented. However, the distraction of the flowers was brief.

As a family, we paused ever so briefly at the threshold of the viewing room. Though silent, I was desperate to summons the strength and composure necessary to face this dreaded moment. As Ricky led us into the room, my eyes were immediately drawn the length of the room to the casket. As if pulled by some invisible magnetic force, I walked directly, without hesitation, to the casket. In it laid Daddy's body.

Through predictable tears, I studied his face, his hands, his body. In my mind, I was unable to determine if he looked older or younger than his sixty years. I simply saw the image of my father, lying there as if sleeping peacefully in his favorite recliner. It was an image that I was comfortable with, but one that I had not expected. Without thought or plan to do so, I found myself stroking his hands, his face, his hair. The warmth of life was gone from his body. As I stood over the body of the man who was my father, I recalled the New Testament scriptural promise that declares, *"To be absent from the body, is to be present with the Lord."* I knew Daddy's personal faith to be strong and secure. With that knowledge, in that moment, I felt a measure of peace. A peace that surpassed my ability to fully understand it. As I leaned over and kissed his forehead, I was no longer afraid of that which I could not explain.

During the next several hours, family, friends and neighbors alike made their way to the funeral home. Temporarily, our individual grief was replaced by our personal responsibility. I, along with Mom, my sister Ellen and my brothers Mark and Dan, greeted each and every person who came. And come they did. From near and far. Many arrived early and stayed late.

At one point during the early evening, as we stood talking to the assembled well-wishers, I felt a hand gently grip my elbow. I turned to find Ricky Morgan standing close to me. When he realized he had my attention, he leaned toward me and whispered in my ear.

"Phil, I don't know how to say this to your mother, but y'all shouldn't be spendin' quite so much time talkin' to each visitor."

The tone of his voice was compassionate, yet his words were direct and to the point. For that very reason, they troubled me.

"Whatta ya mean, Rick?" I asked, searching for more

information.

"Phil, ya may not know it, but there are a lot of people outside who've been waitin' for almost two hours to come by the casket to speak to your mom and you kids. They can't get in. It's too crowded."

I immediately looked up and noticed the throng of people before me. For some reason, I simply hadn't noticed the large number of people before. Or if I had, I hadn't given it any conscious thought.

"There's a line that stretches all the way through the front door and quite a ways down the sidewalk," Ricky continued. "Several of 'em are older folks. I think it'd be a good idea for y'all to do your best to speed it up a bit, if ya can."

I understood his words and appreciated them. I assured him that I would speak to Mom. Ricky later told me that the outpouring of visitors to the funeral home that evening was the greatest he had ever seen, with the only exceptions being those few horrible occasions when a local student had been killed in a car wreck and his or her classmates had turned out in mass to acknowledge the loss. In some strange way, Ricky's words served to encourage me. The number of visitors to a funeral home is by no means the true measure of a man or woman's worth. I understood that. Yet, having such a great number of people make a personal effort to acknowledge our loss served to reassure me that they recognized the uniqueness of this man, Joe Van Hooser.

As the evening wore on and we continued to greet and speak with the large number of visitors, my brother Mark approached me.

In a very matter of fact manner he said, "Phil, come with me. I need to tell ya somethin'."

"Mark, we can't go," I protested. "There are still a lot of folks here. We need to stay here and help Mom greet them."

Mark looked at me hard. "I said come with me."

His tone of voice and demeanor, coupled with the obvious fact that he was bigger, heavier and stronger than me helped me quickly make up my mind. I went with him. As we worked our way through and out of the crowded room, Mark led me to a quiet, secluded corner, away from the crowds. He turned to face me.

"What is it, Mark? What's wrong?" I asked.

"Phil, do ya remember what ya said when we were all talkin' last night?"

"What I said? Last night? Mark, I don't have any idea what you're talkin' about."

More insistently, he continued.

"Last night ya said that ya wished something would happen here at the funeral home. Do ya remember what ya said?"

I could tell Mark was serious. I stood for a moment and thought. Finally, it came to me.

"Yeah, I think so. I said that I wished I'd hear a story about Daddy that would make me laugh. Is that what you're talkin' about?"

"That's it," Mark said confidently. "I thought ya'd like to hear what I just heard. Two of Daddy's coffee-drinkin' buddies from the Burger Queen were just now standin' up by the casket talkin'. They didn't know I was behind 'em. Anyway, I heard 'em talkin' about how Daddy had been arguin' with 'em just a few days ago about Kentucky's upcoming Governor's election and who Daddy thought the next governor oughtta be."

Mark's revelation was in no way surprising to me. Daddy had always held strong opinions about politics and all of us knew it. He took his constitutional rights to exercise his opinion through voice and through vote very seriously. He encouraged us to do the same. He especially looked forward to election day. That was one of the few days of the year during which Daddy would make the effort to wake me in the morning. His enthusiasm was always obvious, though not always contagious.

"Boy, the polls are open. Get up and go vote!" would be his first words to me. Then with a mischievous laugh, he would always add, "Remember, always vote early! Ya never know if you're gonna make it through the day!"

As depressing as the thought may have been, its logic made perfect sense to him.

"Yeah, so what?" I asked Mark, still trying to determine the importance of Mark's message for me.

"Well," Mark continued, "I heard one of 'em turn to the other one and say, 'Well, I bet if old Joe woulda known this was gonna happen, he woulda voted absentee!' Phil, they both just laughed and walked away."

I stood looking at Mark for a moment while the impact of his words sank in. Soon, I felt a smile creasing my face. I noticed Mark was smiling, too. A few seconds later we were both laughing. What a thought! A dead man voting from the grave. A dead man having his vote registered by absentee ballot. Daddy's buddies were right, and both Mark and I knew it! It was exactly the kind of story Daddy would have told had he been there to do so. It was exactly the kind of story that would have made him throw his head back and laugh loudly.

Several times over the balance of that evening and the next day I thought about what Mark had told me. Each time it made me smile again. Throughout that period, I told the story to several other friends and family members. Each one who knew Daddy agreed that it "sounded just like him." They laughed, too.

Now several years later I think back on that simple experience and am convinced that through his friends, family members and the people who knew him, Joe Van Hooser's legacy lives on.

And to think, the legacy was solidified in my mind by one simple wish. A final wish for my dad.

"The reward of a thing well done is to have done it."
RALPH WALDO EMERSON

16

Call Me First

The sun was slowly setting in the western sky, as a light breeze kicked up. The gentle, cool offering provided a temporary, but welcome reprieve from the brutal heat and humidity of the day. The month was August. The year, 1969. The place, Princeton, Kentucky. It felt like a good night for baseball.

Baseball had become my first true passion. Since my very first game as an eight year old, four seasons before, I had been hooked. The uniforms, the crowds, the dugouts, the umpires, the competition, the concession stand—I loved everything about the game.

I considered myself especially blessed to live just down the street from Ratliff Park. During the summer months of my childhood, that period while I was still too young to work, but too old to sit around the house all day, I spent many happy, carefree hours there.

A normal summer day for me as a ten or eleven year old started early with a breakfast of Corn Flakes and knock-knock jokes shared with Captain Kangaroo and Mr. Greenjeans. Then I was off to the ballpark with my tools for the day. Those tools included a bat, a ball, my glove, a tennis racquet and a couple of dead or dying tennis balls, all balanced precariously across the handlebars of my Sears Special bicycle. The morning would invariably be spent alternating between playing catch, home run derby or tennis with whoever might be around—friend or foe. The participants never seemed to matter much. These activities would continue until midday, at which time we would return home for lunch and a brief cooling off period. The early afternoon found me being irresistibly drawn back to the ballpark for a repeat of the mornings activities.

Finally, about four o'clock in the afternoon, I would head home, get cleaned up and eat supper. But, the day was not yet over! By six o'clock or so, I was back at the park to either practice, play or to watch someone else practice or play. By nine or nine-thirty in the evening, it was time to call it a day. The schedule played itself out day after day, throughout the summer months. Amazingly, I never seemed to tire of it.

As the end of the baseball season rapidly approached, I began to worry about the future. Oh, I wasn't worried about significant things such as the economy, nuclear war or the price of tea in China. Instead, I worried about my passion. Baseball. I was painfully aware that the end of my Little League career was in sight.

With the arrival of the next baseball season, as a thirteen year old, I would be required to move *up* and *out*. *Up* to the next level, Pony League. And *out* of the friendly surroundings of Ratliff Park, my home field for the past five seasons. As a Pony Leaguer, I would be playing all my games in the spacious, regulation sized American Legion field across the way. I was looking forward to playing on the "big field." I had often day-dreamed about playing there. A field similar in dimension to those inhabited by my sports heroes of the day, Mickey Mantle, Willie Mays and Roberto Clemente. But, I wasn't quite ready to make the move just yet. There was still one thing I desperately wanted to accomplish in Little League.

I was a pretty decent player during my Little League years. I could run, catch and throw with the best of them. I was even a pretty decent hitter. Almost every game I had at least one and often, two or three hits to show for my efforts. Good hits. Solid hits. Singles, doubles and even an occasional triple.

Yeah, I could hit for average, but not for power. In my five Little League seasons, I had not hit even one home run. Not one! Oh, I had hit balls which ended up being kicked, missed and overrun so many times that I was able to circle the bases and score. But, I had never hit an honest-to-goodness, holy cow, there-it-goes, over-the-fence, out-of-the-park home run.

And I wanted to! I felt like I needed to! I secretly worried that if I couldn't do it on a small field like Ratliff Park where the fences were only two hundred feet from home plate, how could I ever hope to hit one on the big field where the fences were more than three hundred and fifty feet away?

The pressure was on. I put it on myself. I had to hit a home run. And I had to do it soon. I just had to! But how? I had done everything physically I knew to do. There was only one possibility remaining. Prayer!

Now, I grew up in church. Therefore, I understood the concept of spiritual communication. I understood that the Bible was one method God had prepared by which He talked to us. I also understood prayer was the method God had prepared and made available for us to talk to Him. As such, the activity of prayer was not to be taken lightly. And I didn't. I was very serious, though not very mature, when I began praying for my greatest *need*.

"God, *please* let me hit a home run before this season is over. Just one. I won't ask for more. I promise. *Please. Please!*"

Over and over. Night after night, I prayed this simple, yet heartfelt prayer. I was too embarrassed, or guilty or both to confide my prayer to others. This was between me and God, and I sure hoped He was listening.

As I stepped out of the dugout on this particular August evening, my team, the Goldenrod Pirates, was facing our nemesis, the Civitan Tigers. As I stood in the on-deck circle, preparing for my time at bat, I looked out toward the mound at the pitcher I would be facing. He was no stranger to me. As a matter of fact, he had been my best friend since we met in third grade. Though friends, we both were competitors, and therefore, the match up was important to both of us.

Before heading to the plate, I stole a glance up in the stands. There they were. Mom and Dad. Sitting together on the top row of the wooden bleachers, just behind our dugout. As was her usual custom, Mom shouted out some words of encouragement to me.

"Awright. Go get 'em, Phil. You can do it. Get us started. C'mon now. Get a hit."

Mom's words were predictable, usually the same. Often repeated over and over. Words she had undoubtedly learned over the years from other parents at countless other games. Mom's intricate knowledge of the game of baseball was not vast. However, what she lacked in sports competency and expertise, she more than made up for in motherly pride and unbridled encouragement.

Daddy was a different story. He loved sports and understood them fairly well. He made a serious effort to be at every game I played. But, during the games, he was not vocal. He was a watcher, not a hollerer. An understated spectator. It was not his nature to display his emotions publicly. He would study the game carefully and then quiz me about specific parts of it later. Therefore, I was not surprised to see him sitting quietly next to Mom, watching me as I approached the plate.

Once in the batter's box, I turned my full attention to the task at hand. I stared out at the pitcher, my best friend, who for the next hour and a half I had mentally transformed into my bitter rival. I concentrated.

"Awright now, Phil. Keep your feet still. Watch the ball all the way. Swing level and don't try to kill it," I kept reminding myself over and over.

With the passing years, I have long since forgotten the game situation involving this particular at bat. For example, I don't recall if there were runners on base. I have no idea what the score was. I can't remember the pitch count. But, there are certain memories about this at bat that are etched in my brain.

I remember vividly the pitcher's windup and delivery. I remember the flight of the ball, straight and fast. I remember swinging hard, but level. Most clearly, I remember with great pleasure hearing the unmistakable crack of wooden bat solidly meeting pitched ball. Then, with great joy and relief, I remember watching the ball arch higher and higher in the sky before it eventually came to rest just beyond the left center field fence.

A home run by mere inches. But, a home run nevertheless!

I was thrilled! I could barely contain myself as I circled the bases, all the while trying hard to project that "adolescence cool" commonly exhibited in many twelve year old males.

In the stands, Mom was under no such restrictions. Joyously, she celebrated openly, jumping up and down, cheering, clapping and generally enjoying the moment. All the while, Daddy just sat there.

When the game was over, Mom and Dad stood waiting at the fence behind the dugout. As I approached, I saw them both smiling broadly.

"Did ya see it?" I asked, knowing full well they did.

"Did we see it? Of course we saw it! We're so proud of you!" Mom said between hugs and kisses.

I looked up at Daddy.

"Boy, ya hit that ball good," he said evenly, with little emotion.

"Tell him what ya did, Joe," Mom interrupted.

"Daddy, what did ya do?" I asked curiously.

"Aw, nothin'," he said.

"Well, I'll tell ya what he did," Mom said excitedly. "As soon as ya hit that ball, everybody knew it was a good hit. Ya could just tell from the sound of it. Well, *almost* everybody around me jumped up to see if it was gonna be a home run or not. Everybody but your daddy, that is. He just sat there, like a knot on a log, watching the ball. But, as soon as he saw the ball go over the fence, he jumped up and screamed, "YEAH!!" and then he sat down real quick again. Everybody around us saw it and started laughin' and teasin' him."

I looked again at Daddy.

He just grinned a big sheepish grin and said, "Boy, ya did good."

That night I lay in bed, reliving the most exciting day in my life, to that point. It was wonderful. A goal realized. A dream come true. A prayer answered.

In the quiet solitude of that room, I closed my eyes and simply said, "Thank ya, God. I couldn't have done it without ya."

As the years passed, I grew older and predictably, more mature. Without realizing it, the significance of the experience of that first home run faded somewhat for me. Oh, I enjoyed reliving the memory of it occasionally. But, after a while, in light of so many new experiences, the event just didn't seem to be all that important any more.

Instead, with each new year, or new phase of my life, I seemed to be bombarded with startling new revelations of things that were critically important. During my high school years, for example, there were issues involving relationships, personal freedom and heightened responsibility. With my college years came intensified lessons in career choice, professional competition and self-sufficiency. In the years immediately following graduation from college, I faced geographic relocation, professional performance and choosing a partner for life. Somehow, the pace of things had increased considerably since those carefree days spent lounging at the ballpark just a few years earlier. I had to deal with a number of things, all considerably more significant than some minor accomplishment in some child's game.

One of the greatest emotional challenges I had to contend with as I progressed from boy to man, was coming face to face with the reality of mortality. From my junior high school years on, I watched closely as my father's heart troubles worsened and his physical condition deteriorated. It was obvious to most of us, especially Daddy, that life, his life, was fragile at best. Because of his condition, in my heart, I felt certain Daddy would not live to be an old man. That realization was difficult for me to handle. Not only did I fear the thought of losing him, I dreaded the thought of life without him. Selfishly, I worried about the possibility that any children I might father in the future would come after their grandfather's time had passed.

These thoughts began long before I was emotionally ready to commit to parenthood, or even marriage. There was so much I wanted to do—that I needed to do—first. I came to realize, in a very real way, that my current situation was much like my situation from years before. I could easily foresee a time when I would be playing on a "bigger field," no longer in the comfortable confines of life as I had come to know it over the first twenty-five years of my life. The rules would be different. The players would be different. The expectations would be different. I felt the pressure beginning to build. To a large degree, of course, the pressure was self-imposed. Nevertheless, I simply didn't know what to do. It was about that time that I rediscovered my companion from years gone by. Prayer.

It's not that I had forsaken prayer. I hadn't. It's just that it had been a long time since I had realized there was something that I needed badly, that I had absolutely no control over. Such situations call for prayer.

"Dear God, forgive the selfishness of this prayer," I prayed. "But, ya know all things and therefore, ya know Daddy's condition. I simply, but earnestly, pray that ya *please* allow my father to live long enough for my wife, whoever she may be, and I to present him with a grandson. *Please God*, this is my simple prayer."

I prayed this prayer night after night from my college dorm room, to my first apartment, to my honeymoon suite. The words of the prayer may have differed slightly on occasion, but the intent and passion behind each and every prayer were always the same. I prayed the prayer when Daddy was enjoying relatively good health and I prayed it on those occasions when I was called to his hospital bed. I prayed the prayer long before I had identified a woman with whom I wanted to share my life and I continued to pray the prayer after Susan and I were married. All the while, Daddy just kept on plugging.

In August, 1986, Susan and I received some thrilling news. We were going to be parents the following spring. Somehow, I felt a level of confidence, bordering on peace, with the anticipation of the child's arrival. I kept thinking to myself, "I hit that home run before the season was over, didn't I?"

Though we never had an ultrasound to confirm the fact, I

knew in my mind from day one that the baby would be a boy. Not everyone agreed. Many of our friends, neighbors and even total strangers assured us that Susan was carrying a little girl. How did they know? According to them, by the way Susan was carrying the child—high, low or somewhere in between. I could never remember which. The nurses at the doctor's office privately predicted a little girl. Why? Something to do with the baby's heart rate. Even Susan herself had moments of doubt.

I remember a quiet evening at home somewhere around the eighth month of the pregnancy. For months, I had been telling anyone who would listen that Susan and I were having a little boy. How did I know, they would ask. I just knew, I assured them. I was so sure, so confident, I would not even engage in discussing with Susan *possible* names for a daughter.

On this particular evening, Susan and I sat watching television and reading the paper, respectively. After a while, Susan broke the silence.

"Phil, can I ask ya something?"

"Sure, go ahead," I responded, not looking up from my paper.

Ever so sweetly, she continued.

"Phil, you do realize that it's possible that this baby just might be a little girl, don't ya?"

Slowly I lowered my paper to my lap, while turning to face her. I looked deep into the green eyes of the mother of my child and said, "ABSOLUTELY NOT! THIS BABY IS GONNA BE A BOY AND I CAN'T BELIEVE THAT YOU'D EVEN THINK OTHERWISE FOR A MINUTE!"

In shocked disbelief, she stared at me for a moment, eventually shaking her head slightly and returning to her television program.

As the time for the baby's arrival drew near, we were in almost daily contact with family members back in Kentucky. We had determined that we didn't want anyone with us in Florida until after the baby came. So the calls came regularly from family members seeking progress reports. During one of these calls, Daddy got on the phone.

"Boy, are ya ready?" he asked.

"I guess I'm as ready as I can be," I replied.

"Well, I know everything is gonna go good for y'all. But, Phil, I'd like to ask ya to do me a favor."

This statement immediately struck me as being a little odd. First, Daddy wasn't the favor-seeking type. Secondly, it was not his habit to call me "Phil." For as long as I could remember, he had almost always referred to me as "boy."

"Sure, Daddy, what is it?" I asked curiously.

"Phil, I know that y'all will call us as soon as that baby gets here. Ya know your momma'll be dyin' to hear. But, Phil, if that baby happens to be a little boy, will ya call and tell me first?"

Somehow, I understood immediately.

"Sure, Daddy. I promise."

A few days later, in the early morning hours of March 7, 1987, Susan gave birth to a healthy, eight pound, four ounce baby. A baby boy! Watching my son make his entrance into this world was the single most exciting moment I've ever experienced. Even more exciting that hitting my first home run.

Less than twenty minutes after the baby's arrival, I called my parents from the pay phone in the maternity ward. The hour was early, and I knew they would still be in bed. They were. The phone rang several times before Mom finally answered.

"Hello?" was the sleepy, yet enthusiastic reply. She knew that every phone call brought with it the possibility of good news.

"Hi, Mom," I replied.

Unable to contain herself, she blurted out her question.

"Phil, do *we* have a baby?"

I hesitated slightly before answering. I remembered my promise to Daddy.

"Mom, I really need to talk to Daddy," I said with as much self control as I could muster.

"Okay," she said, turning her attention to Daddy. "Joe, get up. It's Phil. He wants to talk to you!"

A few seconds later, I heard that familiar voice on the other end.

"Hey, boy," was his simple greeting.

"Daddy, I promised I'd let ya know. We've got a baby. A baby boy!"

There were a couple seconds of delay in his response as he relayed the news to Mom. Finally, he returned his attention to me.

"Oh, that's good. That's real good," was his response. "Phil, ya got yourself a boy. Is he doin' okay?"

"He's fine."

"How about Susan?"

"She was a trooper. A real baby machine. Daddy, would ya like to know what we named him?"

"Yeah. Sure."

"We named him Joseph Aaron Van Hooser. We're gonna call him Joe."

A long silence fell over the telephone line. I would have loved to have shared the news in person. I knew he would be surprised. Finally, he spoke up again. His voice was cracking.

"Joseph Aaron Van Hooser," he repeated. "And you're gonna call him Joe. That's good, that's real good." He paused again as his voice filled with emotion once more. Finally, he said simply, "Thanks, boy. Here, ya better talk to your momma now."

That night I laid in my bed, reliving the most exciting day of my life. It was wonderful. A goal realized. A dream come true. A prayer answered.

In the quiet solitude of my room, I closed my eyes and simply said, "Thank ya, God. I couldn't have done it without ya."

The very next day a package arrived addressed to "Joseph Aaron Van Hooser." I recognized the handwriting immediately as Daddy's. When I opened the package, I found a thank you note, I'm sure one of the few Daddy ever wrote, which read exactly as follows:

3/7/87

To my first Grandson Joe by the Van Hooser name.

Little one you sure have things rocking this morning. The sun is shining. 40 degrees.
This makes me just a little bit taller this morning. And always remember to keep that name pretty high.
All of my grand kids are very special. But you are the first by the name.
Thank you Phil & Susan.

All my love,
Pa Joe

With the note was a two-blade Case XX pocketknife, with a bone handle. One that Daddy may very well have traded for in the basement of the Caldwell County Court House. It was just like old times. The cycle had repeated itself.

"Destiny is not a matter of chance; it is a matter of choice. It is not a thing to be waited for; it is a thing to be achieved."

WILLIAM JENNINGS BRYANT

EPILOGUE

Joseph Phillip Van Hooser died in his sleep during the e. morning hours of October 26, 1987.

I miss my father. I trust that all who knew him do. He a: so many others like him taught me valuable lessons for li' Their memory and spirit live on in me. For all who rea understand and find value in the lessons in this book, I hop the same is true.

I'm proud to be "Joe's boy." I pray that I will be able to live my life with such faith, courage, honesty, integrity and commitment that my son will one day be proud to be "Phil's boy." If so, the legacy has continued.

May God richly bless you in your journey.

All the best!

Phillip Van Hooser
"Joe's boy"

———

*"Look how far I've come
to get back where I started from."*
WAYLON JENNINGS